OFFLINE REBEL

THE BOLD MAGIC OF LIVING WITHOUT A SMARTPHONE

FLORA HOPE LONDON, M.A.

CONTENTS

Unlight the Dark   vii
Author's Note   ix
Introduction   xi

Part I
RECLAIM THE MAGIC
1. What's Your Boldness IQ?   3
2. Wake the Genius   17
3. You Have No New Notifications   29
4. Books & Blurbs   43
5. Connect the Dots   55
6. Rearview Mirror   69

Part II
CREATE NEW MAGIC
7. Screen-Free Living Spree   81
8. Velvet Joy   93
9. Emerald Green   103
10. Artist's Cobblestone Path   115
11. Mind & Body in Synch   127
12. The Golden Egg   141

Part III
LIVE YOUR MAGIC
13. Top 10 Benefits of Living without a Smartphone   151
14. The Offline Rebel Three-Week Action Plan   153
15. THE ULTIMATE CHALLENGE   161
    100 Fun & Creative Offline Ideas   163

Afterword   169
Acknowledgments   171
Notes   173

To You – This is my love letter to all who seek to live more fully, more boldly, and more authentically

*

To My Mother, Joan – thank you for passing on a love of writing, for your mentorship, and for always believing in me, even when my ideas seem crazy

*

In Loving Memory of My Father, Victor – who taught me the joy of reading and the value of honest work

*

In Honor of Anne LaBastille – the original offline rebel and my personal heroine

UNLIGHT THE DARK

Into the dark
To find the light
Unplugged
To connect
Sun, moon, stars
The only illuminations
Unlight the dark
Untouched thoughts
Free, wild
Into the dark
Ascend
From the glare
Resting weary eyes and mind
No inhibitions, no restrictions
Unglued but not unhinged
Into the dark
See more clearly
The moonlit water of the ocean
Speaks in an ancient voice most can no longer hear.

AUTHOR'S NOTE

I wrote this book in 2019 when smartphones were at the height of their popularity and more than 80 percent of the American population owned one. As we move forward into the next decades, it is likely that other forms of mobile technology will edge the smartphone out of its first place reign. Smartwatches, virtual reality glasses, and artificial intelligence voice assistants are just a few of the contenders. Whenever and wherever this book finds you, even if it is one hundred years from now, you can still apply the principles of offline rebellion. You can create the bold magic to thrive as our ancestors did for millennia without the mobile device *du jour*.

INTRODUCTION

BIRTH OF A REBELLION

"The only way to deal with an unfree world is to become so absolutely free that your very existence is an act of rebellion."
- Albert Camus

The cellular signal died halfway through my one hundred fifty-mile journey crossing the state of Florida from west to east. Even though it was a cool February day, I started to sweat. There were no houses or businesses along this rural stretch of road, only horse and cattle farms, lush palm trees, sweet orange groves. Under other circumstances, I would have basked in my idyllic surroundings, but alone and cut off from the online world, I couldn't focus on anything but lurking danger.

Panic assaulted me as my imagination invented frightening scenarios. What if my aging 2007 Toyota Corolla broke down? What if I drove over a jagged rock and slashed a tire? What if I lost the way and wound up stranded in a sketchy ghost town? As I shook my iPhone 8 in a futile attempt to regain the signal, I felt a sensation of being airborne. In one careless instant my car had jumped from smooth pavement to lumpy grass. Gasping, I jerked the steering wheel to the left to avoid the deep ditch that would have incapacitated my vehicle. As this was Florida, that ditch could very well have been a deadly sinkhole.

Back on the two-lane country road, I slowed the car to a stop and parked on the non-existent shoulder. I hadn't seen another car for at least twenty miles, so I didn't worry too much about my precarious location. Inhaling a shaky breath, I realized that my dependence on the smartphone could have killed me. I had become so conditioned to having online tools at my access that I couldn't survive for a few minutes without them. Or at least that's what I believed. In the weeks and months to come, I learned that I didn't need a smartphone at all. And you might not either.

Common Problem, Uncommon Solution

Where is your smartphone right now? Chances are it's either on you or less than six feet away from you. And it's distracting you as you read this. The very presence of a smartphone has proven to steal our attention from work tasks, social interactions, and creative pursuits.[1] So, as you embark on this maverick journey as an Offline Rebel, commit to turning your phone off and keeping it as far away as possible (Antarctica would be preferable).

There is a desperate but silent need sweeping across society: to awaken and appreciate each irreplaceable moment. In the sage words of the Dalai Lama: "Every day, think as you wake up, today I am fortunate to be alive, I have a precious human life, I am not going to waste it." That's great advice, but how often do we follow it in this era of breakneck speed and high definition greed? Smartphones enable us to live on autopilot, not paying any mind to the bounty of the present. Ironically, the newfangled concept of FOMO (fear of missing out) contributes to smartphone overuse when what we're actually missing out on is our real lives.

For me, the solution was simple but dramatic: relinquish my smartphone and regain my life. To that unorthodox proposition, you probably have a legitimate response – why not just spend less time using the phone?

I knew I could experiment with a gimmicky forty-eight-hour or thirty-day technology fast, but I also knew that I would probably gain all the weight back. Smartphones are feather light giants, but mostly they are *giants* and not readily defeated. In truth, the addiction may be in the design. Silicon Valley insider and former Mozilla employee Aza Raskin told BBC News in 2018:

> It's as if they're taking behavioural cocaine and just sprinkling it all over your interface and that's the thing that keeps you coming back and back and back. Behind every screen on your phone, there are…literally a thousand engineers that have worked on this thing to make it maximally addicting.[2]

If that's not scary enough, Facebook's founding president, Sean Parker, has even admitted that in forming a business model, his company was "exploiting a vulnerability in human psychology," and that they "understood this consciously and we did it anyway."[3] One of the most addictive techniques that engineers have developed is infinite scroll. If you've ever swiped through a social media feed and wondered when all the new photos and stories would end, then you've been a chess piece in the game of infinite scroll. In between all that online junk mail are subliminal (and not so subliminal) messages from advertisers, urging us to try their product or service. But since we're addicted, we don't always notice and the mindless scrolling continues.

Is the term "addiction" too strong to characterize the impact of smartphones and social media apps? Well, consider another contemporary fixation: video games. The World Health Organization (WHO) defines Gaming Disorder as "impaired control over gaming, increasing priority given to gaming over other activities to the extent that gaming takes precedence over other interests and daily activities, and continuation or escalation of gaming despite the occurrence of negative consequences."[4] If video games have been deemed addictive, then their smartphone counterparts may not be far behind. Further, the WHO's definition of Gaming Disorder contains haunting shadows of the behaviors that smartphones and social media elicit.

If we are addicted, then technology mavens have us exactly where they want us. The more time we spend online, the more money we shove into the fat wallets of the digital drug dealers. That $1,000 smartphone is only the starting point. We have to dress up our devices, cloak them with screen protectors, accessorize them with flashy cases, and prop them up on adjustable stands. Then, there's the money that we're not always aware of – the millions of dollars that data mining companies and online advertisers pour into the mobile industry wagering that we'll never defeat that giant. Like cereal brands marketing their sugary junk to unwitting children, technology companies are hypnotizing us with their shimmering gold timepieces. Fortunately, I realized that it was up to me to grab the manipulative stopwatch, throw it to the ground, and crush it.

Who Am I and Why Did I Write This Book?

I fit into that hazy cohort sandwiched between Generation X and the Millennials, a demographic dubbed the Xennials and born roughly from the late 1970s to the early 1980s. The only screens in our childhoods projected educational film strips, Saturday morning cartoons, cheesy evening sitcoms and perhaps a nonviolent Nintendo game or two. We spent the vast majority of our formative years exploring the tangible world: playing hopscotch outside until sunset; riding bikes and roller skating; dashing through sprinklers on scorching summer days.

However, I do not believe that everything was better in the "good ol' days." Give me a white board and dry erase marker over a dusty blackboard and screeching chalk any day. And how annoying was it to adjust those temperamental antennas on the television every five minutes? Not everything in the pre-digital era is worth praising, but there's no debating that it was a starkly different world for the Xennials (and anyone born before us).

A once simple world shapeshifted into a digital galaxy during the Xennials' young adulthood, introducing us to a lightning-paced way of life that was non-existent in the analog ease of the 1980s and 1990s. Today, most of my generation has acclimated to leaving the 20th century in the rubble and fully adopted a digital identity while I have happily rebelled.

I've always been more Wilma Flintstone than Jane Jetson. The last among my college friends to buy a cell phone, I finally capitulated halfway through 2001 but didn't text until nearly a decade later. I was also the last of my peer group to get a smartphone, reluctantly leasing one at the end of 2015 and wondering what all the fuss was about. I could barely read the microscopic words on the glaring screen, let alone whittle away hours each day staring at the frustrating contraption. But that soon changed.

By 2016 I was compulsively checking my phone every ten minutes and wasting an obscene amount of time scrolling through tabloid news stories and social media feeds even though I didn't have any active profiles of my own (yes, I was a lurker). My health paid the price as I developed almost daily tension headaches accompanied by pain behind my eyes and cramps throughout the entire length of my arms. Even when I did a "digital detox" and shut the phone off for a few hours, the symptoms persisted. Does any of this sound familiar?

Worse than the physical damage was the mental destruction. As a freelance writer, my ability to focus is non-negotiable yet I couldn't manage to sit at my computer for a half hour without checking my phone. Unfinished projects rotted in my mind and collected invisible dust.

My mobile dependency launched a domino effect as I found myself:

- Checking my phone immediately upon waking, even if it was only 4:30 am
- Fighting temptation to check it if I woke up in the middle of the night
- Scrolling through emails while talking (and supposedly listening) on the phone
- Spending far less time on valuable hobbies like reading, journaling, and exploring the outdoors
- Becoming dependent on my GPS apps and not paying attention to where I was going
- Browsing and shopping online even when there was nothing I needed
- Over-consuming news stories and falling into depression

Before I untethered my body and brain from the smartphone shackles, I experimented with different strategies to reduce my screen time:

- Keeping my phone off and buried under a pillow in the living room at night
- Turning the phone off for a designated period during the day
- Leaving home without the phone

I even scrawled on neon Post-it notes and stuck them strategically throughout my apartment. Peppering the messages with expletives, I shouted at myself in capital letters to put the phone down. But I would shred those notes rather than heed them. Something wasn't computing. Every effort I made to reduce my smartphone usage was either a failure or a temporary Band-Aid. As soon as I was in the presence of that compelling little rectangle again, I would revert to my destructive habits. Did I lack self-control? Was it a flaw in my personality that kept me glued to my smartphone?

Psychologists and scientists debate these questions, with some claiming that smartphones spawn the addictive behavior previously discussed while others chalk it up to obsessive-compulsive tendencies. Regardless of the diagnosis, I knew that the quality of my life could skyrocket without a smartphone and all its frivolous distractions.

A Life-Changing Decision

In early 2019 I read how Vitaminwater had enticed one Millennial with $100,000 to give up her smartphone for a year. Energized by this woman's boldness, I decided to banish the monkey on my back without the lure of a 100K payday. Why? Because my sanity and health have no price tag (and neither do yours). So, I gave up my smartphone not for an hour, a week or a year, but indefinitely.

Just as I have always been an old soul, I have also been a rebellious one. I have survived without health insurance for almost fifteen years. I refuse to work a nine to five job even though my freelance career is as unpredictable as the path of a tornado. On a whim, I moved more than one thousand miles from home to a state where I knew a grand total of two people. Experiences mean much more to me than material comforts. In a nutshell, I never liked the music of 1990s alternative rock band Rage Against the Machine, but I sure dug the concept.

Therefore, it was with great pleasure that I kissed my smartphone goodbye. The sensation of freedom was immediate and powerful. It was as though an albatross had released an unbreathable grip over my life. Unreachable and mysterious, I felt like an incognito spy prowling the streets for adventure. The aches and pains subsided and my mind was clear and light. I felt so good that I knew I needed to share my story to help others who may feel, as I did, that the smartphone addiction was helpless.

What to Expect in This Book

Offline Rebel: The Bold Magic of Living Without a Smartphone illustrates how amazing you can feel too, how much you can accomplish, how engaged you can be with your loved ones, and how you can improve every aspect of your life by relinquishing this modern convenience that has been sold to us as a necessity.

Could you do it? Could you swim away from the virtual vortex and dive headlong into reality by giving up your treasured phone? Call it extreme digital detoxing. Call it crazy. But no matter what you call it – your life *will* change and you *will* grow if you undertake this challenge. But the choice is yours and it may not be an obvious one.

Smartphones have become as ubiquitous as clothing and not owning one may make some people feel naked. In turn, owning a smartphone means dressing to the nines while succumbing to peer, corporate and media pressure. The initials of Offline Rebel remind us that we have more than one option. Are you going to drown yourself in digital media OR are you going to take a stand and risk standing out? Are you ready to make a change OR do you prefer the status quo? Are you a renegade OR a follower?

There are no right or wrong answers, only choices. This book is not a one-size-fits-all T-shirt and you may find that it is enough to modify your screen time rather than send your smartphone packing. (But I would remind you about that yo-yo digital dieting and rebound weight gain.)

Offline Rebel is organized into three distinct sections:

Part One addresses the burning question: Why would anyone want to give up her smartphone for a day, let alone long-term? I'll share how my life has improved since going smartphone-free and how your life could improve too.

Part Two explores the riches that the offline world has to offer, reconnecting you with your creative side and helping you thrive mentally, physically, and spiritually. You might be amazed at what you can accomplish and enjoy without the dubious constant companion of a mobile device.

Part Three provides further tools: the top ten benefits of living without a smartphone; a focused Offline Rebel Three-Week Action Plan with baby steps and giant leaps; plus a fully offline list of enjoyable things to do.

Sprinkled throughout this book are reflective questions, interactive exercises and offline solutions that will guide you to redefine your relationship with technology into one that puts you in the driver's seat. If you feel that your smartphone has a vice squeeze over your life right now, you'll be equipped with the tools to take the reins by the end of this book.

Beyond the smartphone, this book also aims to illustrate what we gain from spending as much time offline as possible.

For so many of us, including myself, technology is unavoidable in the workplace. But we have infinitely more control over how we occupy our free time. From the dramatic thrill of horseback riding in the wilderness to the simple pleasure of reading a novel on a rainy afternoon, *Offline Rebel* journeys to places where mobile devices only get in the way.

Finally, *Offline Rebel* is not just for you but for your children if you're a parent (or a concerned aunt, uncle, grandparent, godparent, etc.). We know intuitively that our comparatively screen-free childhoods were healthier than the digital overload children absorb today. But why? We'll hear from experts in the fields of psychology, sociology, technology and medicine to illuminate why young people should not have smartphones. We'll also hear stories from among the 20 percent minority of Americans who don't have smartphones to understand why they prefer to live tech-lite.

At its core, this book is not about giving up or losing anything. This book is a cordial invitation to find and gain your peace.

PS: Is your smartphone still on?

I

RECLAIM THE MAGIC

"Technology is cool, but you've got to use it as opposed to letting it use you."
- Prince

WHAT'S YOUR BOLDNESS IQ?

"Go confidently in the direction of your dreams! Live the life you've imagined. As you simplify your life, the laws of the universe will be simpler."
-Henry David Thoreau

CINCO DE MAYO is a celebration of the Mexican Army's victory over the French Empire, but I found myself feeling festive on that date over a different sort of rebellion. May 5, 2019 marked my first full day without a smartphone (or any cell phone for that matter). The day before, I had surrendered my leased iPhone 8 to the carrier store where I shelled out a small fortune to break my contract. But it was worth every dollar.

That night, I slept better than I had in months (years?) falling into a deep slumber at 10 pm and only stirring once versus the three or four times I would wake up when I was under smartphone domination. Amazingly, my body was already producing the melatonin it needed for a restful night's sleep.

In the morning I awoke refreshed and started the day with a brisk thirty-minute stroll around the lake near my apartment rather than by fusing to a touch screen. My senses were heightened as I listened to the calls of Florida sea birds and soaked in the shifting rose and lavender clouds in the sky. Back inside I sat down to a leisurely breakfast of steel cut oatmeal, walnuts and cinnamon before drifting to my desk to begin my work day of writing and editing natural health articles.

Better quality sleep and a tranquil morning ritual were just two of the notable changes that marked my first week of freedom:

- I also felt calmer throughout the day and my heart no longer palpitated with anxiety.
- I didn't miss the non-communication method of text messaging. Not for one single second. Note: I chose to free myself of *all* mobile devices, including an ordinary cell phone. I am not suggesting that you do the same, unless you really want to go rogue!
- Going out became an off-the-grid adventure even if I was just having lunch at my favorite café a few miles from home. *Catch me if you can...oh wait, you can't*, I thought with a smirk.
- Talking on my new landline made phone conversations a pleasure again as I could hear people more clearly through hard-wired technology than I could through a crackling wireless connection.
- I immediately became more productive, devoting hours to writing projects that once would have

been squandered scrolling through the bottomless black hole of cyberspace.

- Whereas I had once slipped into the woodwork as a hermit writer, I now immersed myself in the community. I trained to be a volunteer at an animal shelter; joined a gym and an indoor volleyball league; and attended church for the first time in eons, also daring to become a choir member and fulfill a lifelong dream to sing.
- My long neglected yoga practice experienced a resurgence as I had the patience to roll out the mat and devote an hour to the discipline each evening.

AND THESE WERE JUST the changes I observed during the *first week* of living without any mobile device other than my laptop. Liberty tasted sweet. Sweetness is contagious. Initially, my family and friends had been skeptical of my decision, warning me that I was putting my safety at risk and moving backwards in time. Some even predicted that I wouldn't last a week without my iPhone. These same people who had mocked my decision to ditch the smartphone now wistfully wondered aloud if they could do the same thing. Could they experience deeper peace and more radiant health by losing less than six ounces? Could you?

Yes, it is possible for you to invite an abundance of peace, health (and unexplored creativity!) into your life. The question is *will* you do it? Are you willing to give up the conveniences of your smartphone in exchange for the priceless rewards that come through living as a trailblazer?

It took me about six months of mulling the decision over before I finally executed it. I was resistant at first because the iPhone seemed to spoon feed so many features that I *had to have* (a widely held misconception that Apple may be banking on). Here are my top five smartphone conveniences that I falsely believed I couldn't live without:

1. GPS. When I was seventeen and a novice driver, I would quip that I could get lost in a phone booth. Over the years, that joke lost its relevance, but I maintained my poor sense of direction. So now the punchline is that I could get lost in my own apartment. Therefore, the navigation apps on my smartphone seemed indispensable. Like the characters in one of the great road trip movies of the 1980s, *Lost in America*, I found myself in remote and occasionally unsettling areas without a GPS. Other times while I was "lost" I was reminded of how beautiful this country is, especially my southern corner in Florida where palm trees sway and citrus groves flourish. Slowly I learned to find my way without a GPS. I started observing and memorizing landmarks, getting to know my neighborhood better in one month than I had in two years of living there and leaning on technology. My sense of direction wasn't as bad as I thought once I greased up the wheels and started using it.

2. Email. Having the ability to check my email anytime and anywhere, even on the beach, had once seemed like a gift. But constant availability is a double-edged sword, never permitting us to fully relax and unburden ourselves of thoughts about work. As long as I answered my emails within one business day, what was the big rush? Yes, I am a freelancer (which translates as almost-unemployed-hippie-dreamer-one-client-check-away-from-living-in-a-van-down-by-the-river), but I still needed time to decompress as we all do.

3. Camera. Though I'm not one to pout and pucker like Daisy Duck for selfies, I did like snapping shots of random flowers and wildlife. So, I dug into the bottom drawer of my dresser, dusted off my digital camera circa 2010 and popped it in my purse. Problem solved. I didn't take as many photos with the digital camera as I had with the smartphone, but that turned out to be a blessing in disguise as I focused more fully on experiencing each moment.

4. LoseIt. This calorie tracking app helped me shed twenty pounds in three months and I was afraid to live without it. Visions of caramel hot fudge sundaes and baked Brie cheese wedges filled my head as I worried that my eating would get out of control again. Then I discovered that the app also has a fully functional website, so I was able to continue monitoring my eating habits to maintain my weight. (On a cheat day I did make a pit stop at Dairy Queen and couldn't help but smile at the printed words on my ice cream cone's paper wrapper: "The Ultimate Mobile Device." Indeed.) On the same token, I could no longer track the number of steps I walked each day without an investment in a pedometer. An offline solution fixed this dilemma as I lost myself in long strolls, far from any technology that would interrupt my communion with the great outdoors.

5. Music. Digital music has been a great victory for the environment, eliminating the need for wasteful plastic "jewel" CD cases and fuel-burning deliveries. My music apps contained over two thousand songs that I was reluctant to part with – but again, laptop computer to the rescue. I also unearthed a radio/sound machine that projected ocean waves and raindrops for those deafening nights that only apartment dwellers can understand. Using the radio for the first time felt like coming home – I loved the staticky imperfection of the FM stations, much like Frank Barone craved the scratchy sounds of his vintage record player on an episode of *Everybody Loves Raymond*. Plus, is there anything quite like cruising down the highway with the windows rolled down and the radio cranked up?

Offline Solution #1: *What would your top five must-have list look like? Rank your favorite smartphone features/apps and then brainstorm an alternative for each.*

PERHAPS IT WAS EASIER for you to fire off the five apps you can't live without than it was for you to dream up replacements for them. That's OK. As we voyage together, we will see how naturally we can access our innate resourcefulness and devise solutions when technology is taken out of the equation.

In fact, successful brainstorming has been our second nature all along, but we have neglected this human skill and passed it over to our handheld computers. In the words of Peter Sagal, author of *The Incomplete Book of Running*:

> We evolved in very different circumstances than what we are living in now; to be attentive to the world and not with a screen in front of us. The reason we are up on two legs is so that we can look around and think. We're supposed to ruminate. We didn't evolve these extraordinary brains and self-consciousness so we could outsource our thinking. Anybody who has done creative work knows what's needed to do that is uninterrupted thought.[1]

As we will discover, the creative work that Sagal mentions is not exclusive to artists. We all have creative facets to our personalities which lay dormant when we're letting our devices do the creating: manufacturing artificial environments, virtual friends, and low cognition games that drain our mental energy without stimulating our minds. As children, we are constantly creating by coloring outside the lines, inventing fairy tale worlds, telling whimsical stories, and shaping mounds of Play-Doh. Creativity has become lost in the mix of adulthood, especially since the advent of smartphones that often serve as pacifiers for kids and grown-ups alike.

Recreating Childhood

Every day I walk through the concrete breezeway of my apartment building and find the neighbors' elementary age children with phones rather than books in their curious hands. Unaware of their surroundings, the children come perilously close to the staircase, also made of concrete, as their mother trails behind them entrenched in her own virtual universe. I have attempted to offer a neighborly hello to this family on more than one occasion, but they never seem to hear me.

These children will grow up without having known the kind of carefree playtime that every previous generation knew. They will not have a frame of reference to understand how damaging their online behaviors are. These youngsters belong to the aptly named generation of Digital Natives (alternately called Generation Z). What will happen to play and imagination in the future when multiple generations of Digital Natives have grown older and are raising their own children with wireless babysitters? They might need to go against the grain and acknowledge that children should not be spending their crucial development years in front of screens.

But don't take my word for it. The World Health Organization (WHO) issued new guidelines in 2019 regarding how much screen time children under the age of five should be allowed. For babies under two years old, the WHO contends that no screen time at all is appropriate. From age two to four, the WHO suggests that one hour of daily maximum screen time may be acceptable. The report also advocates for less sedentary time for children, promoting physical activity which may in turn lead to more restful sleep.[2]

Are children actually getting that essential restful sleep? Instead of meditating on bedtime stories and lullabies, some children haul their individual iPads to bed until they fall unconscious. I have a friend who sends his three daughters to bed every night with their Kindles blazing brighter than the stars. The girls, all of whom are under the age of five, have no limitations on their screen time. When I shared the WHO report with my friend over coffee, he shrugged and mused, "It's the only way I can get them to fall asleep." As I am not a parent, I didn't pursue the topic, but I had a hard time believing that these little girls would only go to sleep with tablets in hand – unless those same tablets had been in their little palms all day, thus rendering their brains unable to shut down.

While there may not be specific recommendations for adults, it is safe to say that we would also benefit from as little screen time as possible. If we acknowledge this fact, our well-being may hinge on our willingness to slash our screen time. The average American sleeps just 6.8 hours per night rather than the recommended seven or eight.[3] Energy drink companies have been seizing on the lucrative opportunities of an insomniac nation and will no doubt boost their profits as the average person's nights become even more restless.

Since we're all awake, tell me: what's your boldness IQ? The more willing you are to let go of your smartphone and dive back into life, the higher your boldness IQ. If you're not sure yet whether you would (or could) actually live smartphone-free, my hope is that you will have a fresh outlook by the last page of this book and realize that your online behaviors affect not only you and your adult loved ones but also the children in your life. There's the proverbial golf widow and there's the smartphone orphan, a child whose parents are too enamored with their devices to lend an attentive ear.

Still, you may find the idea of living without a smartphone to be absurd. The pertinent question for me became more of how can I keep living *with* a smartphone when it's detracting so much from my life? Just as I wouldn't keep one foot in an abusive relationship, I decided that I wasn't going to cling to my phone part-time either. Likewise, a substance abuse counselor would not tell an addict to keep the drug around for holidays, anniversaries and birthdays. If you have an irrepressible sweet tooth (like I do) then you're not going to keep a tub of pistachio ice cream in the freezer. We all know that it's impossible to eat just one potato chip. Our taste buds crave the saltiness just as our brains crave the dopamine release that occurs when we learn a new factoid. If we're serious about healthy eating, then, we might clear our pantries of potato chips. If we're committed to healthy living, we might sweep our smartphones out the door.

Drastic action is sometimes necessary to reclaim our most vital assets: a thinking mind, a bloom of creativity, close relationships to others, and most of all, personal peace of mind. However, the fact remains that we still need to communicate and do not dwell in caves. Fortunately, there are several more economical choices than the newest iPhone release.

Affordable Alternatives to Smartphones

Landlines
When I was a kid we quaintly called it "the phone," but the contemporary moniker is "landline." A majority of American homes no longer have landlines, but they can be money savers

for those who do. For starters, home telephones are practically indestructible and therefore a one-time expense that could cost as little as $20. Second, many companies encourage you to bundle landline, Internet, and television at a discounted rate. I have a bundled package (minus the television) with Internet and landline that costs $60 per month including taxes and fees. That number represents more than a 40 percent savings over my former smartphone bill and there is no comparing how much clearer the sound quality is on my landline. Using a smartphone as an actual phone seems to be an afterthought now as reception is often garbled even in cities. Landlines are godsends for those of us who have the gift of gab.

Tablets

A no-bells-and-whistles tablet can be as low as $50 to purchase and exactly $0 per month to maintain. Skype conversations, both audio and video, are free. A tablet easily fits in a purse or briefcase and comes in handy for travel. Other than for travel, though, you might want to keep your tablet powered down for at least twenty-three hours a day. If you don't set such strict limitations on your tablet usage, you could be right back where you started with chronic migraines and techno stress. With careful monitoring, a tablet is the closest substitute to a smartphone. The larger screen is somewhat easier on the eyes and the device has all the functionality of your phone without the horrifying monthly bill.

Basic "Flip" Phones

Ordinary cell phones have devolved and no longer include some of the features that made them innovative in the early 2000s. For example, most flip phones do not have keyboards anymore which makes texting an exasperating and time-consuming ordeal. But if you're not interested in texting and want to keep a mobile phone for emergency purposes or talking, then basic flip phones are inexpensive options. Some basic phone plans cost as little as $10 a month depending on how many minutes and messages you use. Basic phones may feel like outdated station wagons, but paying $10 a month might help you save up for that sleek Mercedes convertible.

Prepaid Mobile Phones

Not many companies are producing prepaid mobile phones, but you can find these rarities if you search online. You can opt for a basic flip phone and probably won't pay more than $100 for your stripped down device. From there, you may purchase a traditional plan or a sort of digital calling card loaded with a set number of minutes. The cards usually expire after ninety days, so if you're not a heavy mobile user, then you might only need to repurchase minutes four times a year. A prepaid mobile phone is a good choice if you favor a no frills emergency line and don't want a hard inquiry into your credit.

Laptops

Laptop computers are more compact and lightweight than ever with some weighing under three pounds. They offer most of the conveniences of a smartphone without as much risk of overuse and boundary crossing. (When was the last time you brought your laptop to the movie theater?) While many people run businesses from their smartphones, I find it easier to work from my laptop with word processing and spreadsheet programs much smoother to navigate with a real keyboard and a larger screen.

One common benefit of these four alternatives to smartphones is that they tend to have longer life spans, which is good for our wallets and the environment. On the surface, these unconventional choices do not provide the one-stop shopping experience of a smartphone. However, if you make a few tweaks (like I did with my top five apps) you may find that these options are more than satisfactory. One caveat:

even I, Wilma Flintstone, will admit that you will not find a better camera in any of these alternatives. Score one for Jane Jetson and Rosie the Robot. From a financial perspective, though, the smartphone emerges as a profound loser.

My Cost Savings in Going Smartphone-Free

Previous Monthly Phone Bill for Leased iPhone, Unlimited Minutes, Texts and Data: **$110**
Current Monthly Phone Bill for Landline Phone and Internet with Unlimited Minutes and Wi-Fi: **$60**
Monthly Savings: **$50**
Annual Savings: **$600**
Savings over 5 Years: **$3,000**

Offline Solution #2: *How much do you spend on your current smartphone individual or family plan? How much would you like to spend? Calculate the monthly, annual, and five-year savings if you (or a member of your household) were to live without a smartphone.*

An Age-Old Story

Are smartphones the only problem? Moreover, are they the origin of the problem? As I delved deeper into my research for this book, I realized that the root cause of our screen fixation originated long before the first smartphone rolled off the assembly line. Our circadian rhythms were already in jeopardy from the time electricity was invented, while our human obsession with projected images stems from the relief of passivity in a complicated and taxing world. Long commute stressed you out? Stretch out on the couch with a mindless sitcom. Had a fight with your spouse? Tune them out by plugging in your ear buds and cackling at frisky cats on YouTube. Each new technological invention has poured kerosene on the original flaming problem that is summed up in four words: a desire to escape. Smartphones are symptomatic of this issue and exacerbate it at a Richter scale level.

The complementary desire to be entertained by any means, even violent or vulgar, is another driving factor behind the explosive popularity of the iPhone and its younger sibling, the iPad. Gladiator contests, bullfighting and Greyhound racing are just a few of the unfortunate spectacles that have drawn massive audiences to arenas over the centuries. Neil Postman explored this ferocious need to be entertained in 1985 in his book, *Amusing Ourselves to Death*. Written against the backdrop of Reaganomics and the glitz of Las Vegas, a city the author says exists only to entertain, *Amusing Ourselves to Death* was a prelude of things to come.

In the first chapter of his book, Postman notes:

As I write, the President of the United States is a former Hollywood movie actor. One of his principal challengers in 1984 was once a featured player on television's most glamorous show of the 1960's, that is to say, an astronaut.[4]

The astronaut was John Glenn, who became the first American to orbit the earth in 1962. Glenn dropped out of the presidential race in March of 1984 but not before he and Ronald Reagan had set the stage for other celebrity candidates to try their luck at politics. A movie star in the White House may have been inconceivable before Reagan's presidency, but somewhere along the line the script was rewritten. Now we are the stars of our own self-directed stories on social media and, more meaningfully, we are all the stars of this particular story. We are all the main character – the protagonist – and screens are the antagonists or the collective villain. We are also the heroes and heroines as only we have the power to illustrate the pages of our personal stories and transform the plot into something bold and wonderful.

To revisit Thoreau's advice: "Go confidently in the direction of your dreams! Live the life you've imagined. As you simplify your life, the laws of the universe will be simpler." No doubt you have come across the first two sentences of that quote, but have you ever contemplated the line that follows? Simplifying our lives makes everything simpler, says Thoreau. A profusion of digital devices has overcomplicated our every waking moment, but we have the authority to eject the intruders and rediscover what really matters.

WAKE THE GENIUS

"It's not that I'm so smart, it's just that I stay with problems longer."
- Albert Einstein

I WAS RIGHT on time and on track, according to the finite wisdom of Google Maps. As I cruised up Interstate 75 North towards Tampa International Airport, the autumn sun was gleaming and traffic was flowing. The radio was playing Tom Cochrane's "Life Is a Highway," one of those songs that makes you feel much cooler than you actually are. I texted my mother, who had just flown in from New York, that I would be there in less than fifteen minutes. Yes, I was an idiot for texting while driving and taking a risk with my life and the lives of other drivers. But I was equally foolish for listening to my GPS which inexplicably went haywire, throwing me off course and booting me from the highway on what I realized too late was the wrong exit.

For reasons I still don't understand, the GPS could not locate me and kept spitting out directions that took me farther and farther from my destination. I thought of my sixty-six-year-old mother waiting expectantly for me at the airport after a year since our last visit. With nothing but my phone to release my frustrations on, I threw the device into the backseat and stopped at a gas station to get directions the tried and true old-fashioned way: by asking a real live person. A friendly employee at the Quick-Mart pointed me in the right direction and with no further "help" from my GPS I arrived at the airport, albeit half an hour late and wholly frazzled.

The most ridiculous thing about this fiasco is that it could have been avoided. The airport was almost entirely a straight route from my starting point, only requiring one turn and one exit. Why didn't I simply write the directions down? Or, better yet, why didn't I memorize them? Because I trusted an app more than I trusted myself. I relied on technology before I channeled the capabilities of my own brain. I had also checked traffic reports before leaving for the airport which, at the time, seemed logical. Later, I reflected on how we always need to be prepared for the unexpected, on the road and in life. Ensuring that the traffic is moving along in neat green lines robs us of a crucial coping mechanism. Information from our smartphones infuses us with a false sense of control, that we can access anything in less time than we can measure. The only barrier is how many bars are visible at the top of our screens, and if the device is operating at top capacity, we may as well be setting off into the stars for that's how far we can travel and no one can stop us. But we might want to disembark the spaceship and let our brains take us for a much more stimulating ride.

Your Brain at the Gym

"EVERY ONCE IN A WHILE, a revolutionary product comes along that changes everything," said Steve Jobs. He wasn't kidding. In less than fifteen years since the iPhone launch in 2007, we have become so dependent on these pocket pests that we have forgotten about the powerful instruments inside our heads that scientists may never fully decode. We lean on our smartphones to tell us everything from simple facts like the time and weather to how much to tip at restaurants, a straightforward calculation that anyone who passed middle school math should be able to do unassisted. Likewise, we can jog our long-term memories to retrieve a known fact rather than searching it up on Google. We can write down notes with pen and paper rather than tapping them onto a screen.

And why would we want to do these things unassisted, you ask? Why overcomplicate our lives when smartphones have seemingly simplified so much? Wouldn't that be a waste of precious time and effort? Well, our micro intellectual efforts may have an effect on the macro efforts that make us successful. In other words, writing notes longhand is one small way we can retrain our brains to slow down and focus for the inevitable times when much greater projects will demand our full concentration. In his book, *Deep Work: Rules for Focused Success in a Distracted World*, Georgetown University computer science professor Cal Newport explains the importance of retained focus:

> To produce at your peak level you need to work for extended periods with full concentration on a single task free from distraction. Put another way, the type of work that optimizes your performance is deep work. If you're not comfortable going deep for extended periods of time, it'll be difficult to get your performance to the peak levels of quality

and quantity increasingly necessary to thrive professionally.[1]

Newport is specifically addressing the workforce as he implies that competition is stiff, so we must differentiate ourselves through the ability to devote our entire attention to one task. In a society that values managing multiple projects like a clown juggles rubber balls, pouring all our concentration into just one task may seem unfathomable. But as the brain's multitasking capabilities have proven to be mythical, we not only need to focus because of a competitor waiting in the wings but also to complete a project successfully for its own merit. We can scatter our brains like dandelion seeds across several projects and reap nothing but weeds, or we can root ourselves into one worthwhile challenge and grow into a stately tree.

Whether we comprise the workforce, the retirement community, or a student body, we should all participate in deep work. Particularly as our brains age, the notion of "use it or lose it" comes into play. Puzzles and brain teasers are enjoyable examples of how to maintain and further develop our brain functioning. I have never been a fan of jigsaw puzzles, especially the maddening ones with 1,001 slippery pieces, but apparently they can be brain savers, especially for people over fifty. One recent study on jigsaw puzzles found that this hobby can be a protective factor for cognitive aging.[2] Enjoying an activity that you did as a kid and keeping your brain young – what could be better? This study focused on the benefits of jigsaw puzzles, but other mind-bending exercises like Sudoku, word searches and mazes could have similar effects, potentially staving off diseases like Alzheimer's.

On the flipside, smartphones are progressively short circuiting our brains. Smartphone overuse interferes with our brain chemistry, sometimes causing depression, anxiety, insomnia and impulsive actions – like reaching out to that ex you haven't spoken to in five years.[3]

Since smartphones are relatively new to humanity, the long term effects are a mystery. One thing is certain: we are cognizant of the damage that our smartphones are inflicting. In her book, *How to Break Up with Your Phone: The 30-Day Plan to Take Back Your Life*, author Catherine Price reveals:

> My attention span is shorter. My memory seems weaker. My focus flickers. Sure, some of this may be due to natural age-related changes in my brain. The more I thought about it, however, the more I began to suspect that there was an external factor at play – and that factor was my phone.[4]

Price also points out how Steve Jobs and Bill Gates placed limits on their own children's technological usage, with the latter not allowing his kids to have phones until the age of fourteen.[5] Chris Anderson, former editor-in-chief of *Wired*, restricts his children's screen time in a similar fashion and says: "We have seen the dangers of technology firsthand. I have seen it in myself. I don't want that to happen to my kids."[6] There are any number of "dangers" to which Anderson could be alluding: propensity for addiction; cognitive weakening; damage to eyesight. If the masterminds of (and experts on) the most popular modern technology are protecting their children from the ills of too much screen time, shouldn't others take the cue? Until we as a society acknowledge and address the problem, our brains will not operate at full capacity.

Just as we exercise our bodies, we must also exercise our brains. A sedentary body weakens, muscles atrophy, endurance wanes. Likewise, a brain coddled by the strong arm of technology will probe its reserves and not find the strength it once had.

Reclaiming Our Brains

In the short term, though, thanks to the plasticity of our brains, we may be able to reverse the damage that smartphones have done simply by relying on artificial intelligence less and stimulating our brains more. Reliance on smartphones slows our thinking abilities and raises levels of cortisol, the chemical popularly known as the "stress hormone." But cortisol levels that have risen due to smartphone overuse will dip when we remove the aggravating variable.

Offline Solution #3: *Take a moment to think of a few ways that you can wake the genius in your everyday life. For example, my reading more than doubled in my post-smartphone life, as I went from reading one or two books a month to the same amount each week. What kinds of cognitive puzzles and activities would you enjoy? Name four challenging games and/or brain boosting goals and commit to trying them all within the next month.*

THOUGH OUR FOCUS in this book is smartphones, we use all kinds of technology as a crutch, which can produce the same undesirable results and undermine our very capable brains. Before there were GPS apps, there were GPS gadgets that mounted inside our cars, bossing us around and sometimes malfunctioning and misleading us in much the same way that today's navigation technology does.

I'll never forget the foggy night in 2011, long before I had a smartphone, when I was driving down a lovely but barren backroad in South Carolina. Without warning, my GPS started giving me directions in Afrikaans, tossing me into alarm because, once again, I had failed to create a back-up plan and take two minutes to scribble the directions on paper. (As you can see by now, navigation technology really doesn't like me.) I drove in circles for an hour as the fog thickened and visibility dwindled. Eventually I reached my destination, exhausted and stressed, but it could have been so much easier had I utilized my own thinking cap. The scarecrow in *The Wizard of Oz* mused, "If I only had a brain," while I brooded, "If I had only *used* my brain."

Whether we value our native intellect more than the programmed intelligence of the smartphone is a matter of perspective: do we view the extra thinking and time as an inconvenience or as a challenge? Easy does not usually mean better, as we learn when we take shortcuts to our goals. Moving sidewalks would be easier on icy January days, but they would do our waistlines no favors.

That night on the labyrinthine roads of rural South Carolina, I learned to shift my perspective from viewing the broken GPS as an unnecessary inconvenience and the choice to use my mind next time as a desirable challenge. Or at least I thought I had. I would learn the lesson all over again when the cellular signal faded during my trek across rural central Florida. That day, when I was inches away from plunging into a ditch (or sinkhole), I had a revelation about my dysfunctional relationship with technology.

I also realized that not one of my close contacts, not even my best friend of eighteen years, has my phone number memorized. I have relatives who would not remember my birthday were it not for their Google reminders. A personal touch? What's that? We would all do well to reacquaint ourselves with the concept yet most American schools no longer teach cursive handwriting, which suggests that as a culture we assign decreasing value to personalization and formality. While we're probably not going to compose missives with fountain pens and parchment paper, it's not too much to ask to learn our loves ones' birthdays by heart – and to wish them well without the intervention of technology.

My friend, Carla, is a high school chemistry teacher and one of the few people I know who still buys stationery. In her early fifties, Carla writes personal notes on paper decorated with cabbage roses and monarch butterflies – because she has the time. The mother of three teenage children and two aging dogs, Carla sends out at least one card a week by her count. Did I mention that Carla owns a flip phone?

"Since I discourage my friends from texting me, I have a lot more time to write to them!" She told me cheerfully.

There are no "happy bday!" messages from Carla on Facebook because she doesn't have a profile. Instead, Carla pores over aisles of Hallmark cards until she finds the perfect greeting to send.

"Everyone always thanks me for sending them a card or note in the mail. I think it surprises them," she shared.

Besides Carla's knack of connecting with those close to her, she recognizes the intellectual benefits of maintaining a basic phone. "I've never had a smartphone, but all my co-workers have one and they can't seem to sit down to focus on grading papers. I don't love marking tests and quizzes in the evenings, but I can easily do it because there's nothing distracting me. I also don't want to lean on artificial intelligence to get me through problems that I could solve myself," Carla said.

With regard to her students, Carla continued, "I've noticed a real decline in how students write over the past twenty years, but especially the past ten years. And I'm not even an

English teacher! Lab reports are littered with silly errors, like a student writing his own name all in lowercase letters."

Text speak is the formal term for the phenomenon Carla has observed. Since today's young people grew up with the Internet, many have adopted the slang, abbreviations, and outright mistakes that the medium perpetuates. The only remedy to this growing problem is for youth to radically decrease their online time and increase their consumption of traditional forms of writing, namely books.

Carla concluded, "They're relying too much on artificial intelligence and it's changing the way they think."

Smartphones do project an astounding level of artificial intelligence, but they certainly make us do stupid things. I see people walking through parking lots with their gazes plunged straight downward to veiled screens that are more protected than they are. Walking while distracted is bad enough, but how about being caught in the middle of a text when the traffic light turns green? With the way people drive these days, we might wonder if we should start wearing helmets and body armor in the car.

Texting while driving is equally as dangerous as putting on lipstick or shaving, yet it seems more socially acceptable. We might point and laugh at someone dipping into a bucket of chicken wings on the road, but we're not very surprised when we see someone typing up a message. It's just normal. I've done it myself and you may have as well. Without going into the depressing statistics about the impact of distracted driving, we can turn the problem around and highlight how enjoyable it is to keep the phone out of sight while on the road.

Offline Solution #4: *Turn your morning commute into the Great American Road Trip by programming a playlist of songs* *that make your spirit soar. Or if you have a low-tech car like I do, listen to the radio and be surprised. Pop in the audio version of a book that you haven't found time to read. If you're like most Americans, you probably drive solo to work, so capitalize on the quiet time and let the messages wait until you arrive at your destination.*

I HAVE ALREADY SHARED one instance when I was foolish enough to text while driving, but here's one more confession. Sometime after my airport mishap, I got myself into a scrape simply by *reading* text messages on my phone. A high maintenance client had been hounding me all day and when three consecutive messages beeped into my phone, I couldn't resist a glimpse. I was driving about forty-five miles per hour in an area of light traffic, so I thought it would be safe to sneak a peek at the messages. Wrong. In the two seconds that I took my eyes off the road, I veered towards the center line and clipped a car on the other side. The driver didn't seem to notice and kept going, but my side view mirror dislodged and crashed to the ground.

That minor incident was a major wakeup call and I never texted while driving again, nor did I so much as look at my phone. Instead, I set the phone to silent and shoved it into my glove compartment before every trip, even a five-minute jaunt to the post office. As I now live without a cell phone, I've become keenly aware of how many people are using theirs while driving. If you've never used your phone while driving, then spread the word of wisdom. If you have, don't let it take an accident (or a tragedy) to smarten up. Besides, it's much more fun to listen up.

Top 10 Driving Songs That Are Better Than Whatever Is Going on with Your Smartphone...

1. I Drove All Night by Cyndi Lauper
2. Born to Be Wild by Steppenwolf
3. Jump by Van Halen
4. Hit the Road Jack by Ray Charles
5. Drive by The Cars
6. Learning to Fly by Tom Petty
7. Roam by the B-52's
8. Little Red Corvette by Prince
9. Everyday Is a Winding Road by Sheryl Crow
10. Shut Up and Drive by Rihanna (that song title says it all, doesn't it?)

Offline Solution #5: *Can you think of a time when technology failed you? How could the situation have been avoided? How can you avoid repeating the situation? Today, try performing one cognitive task that your phone usually does for you. Maybe you'll turn off the GPS or not tap on the calculator.*

Your Amazing Brain

THE HUMAN BRAIN is so central to our existence that it receives 30 percent – nearly a third – of the blood that the heart pumps.[7] Our brains are always working, even when we're in the deepest cycle of sleep, but we apply the brakes to our brains when we zone out with our devices. Your brain was not meant to recline in the passenger's seat or be relegated to co-pilot status. Your brain was meant to drive the car, fly the plane, actively function and grow through life's small everyday incidents that are not as insignificant as they may seem.

In case there are any lingering doubts about how amazing our brains are, here are a few facts to ponder:[8]

- Our brains contain about 86 billion brain cells
- Information travels at about 268 miles per hour through our brains
- We can generate up to 25 watts of electricity in our brains
- Most of us have no less than 50,000 thoughts per day
- The brain's storage capacity may be unlimited (who needs RAM?)

Those are facts about the natural phenomenon that is your brain, not a manmade invention. Our brains are capable of accomplishing wondrous feats if only we would let them.

YOU HAVE NO NEW NOTIFICATIONS

"We will be more successful in all our endeavors if we can let go of the habit of running all the time, and take little pauses to relax and recenter ourselves. And we'll also have a lot more joy in living."
- Thich Nhat Hanh

WHY WOULD a twenty-something senior data analytics consultant from Seattle opt not to have a smartphone? Michael Valeri, who belongs to the generation most likely to own and frequently use a smartphone, answered that question in a 2019 interview with GeekWire. "For me, this feels like the best way I can live my life," Valeri said.[1]

Aside from his professional LinkedIn account, Valeri does not have a profile on any social media sites. His lack of new notifications does not make him feel like an outsider; on the contrary, he enjoys the space and freedom, with one notable exception.

The only time I'll feel disconnected, I'm maybe in a bar or some kind of communal gathering spot, just seeing folks looking at devices. I often imagine a time twenty, thirty years ago where people's heads would be up and observant of people around them and the opportunity to connect with people.[2]

Ironically, it is his mother across the country in Oklahoma who is active on social media and wishes that her son would get online so she could keep up with his everyday life. Valeri, who gets around the Emerald City on an electric bike, prefers to stay anonymous, perhaps because he works in data and knows firsthand how invasive large technology companies can be. In another interview with *The Evergrey*, Valeri explained: "I decided that I didn't want to be part of that data model."[3]

Valeri has good reasons not to want to be part of 'that data model'. The privacy issues that 24/7 connectivity raises are disturbing if not alarming. Every website seems to be tracking us these days, whether we're on mobile devices or desktop computers. Smartphones, however, are especially vulnerable to hackers and privacy invasion because they're perceived as more valuable. After all, we use our phones for everything from banking and bill paying to investing and shopping.

Spyware and viruses are just itching to tap into this treasure trove of confidential information. Dark Caracal is a spyware campaign that started in 2012 and is still going strong. Affecting thousands of smartphone users in more than twenty countries, the campaign employs fake but convincing versions of apps that people unwittingly install on their devices. Once spyware has slithered into your phone, it can find out almost anything about you.

Eva Galperin, cybersecurity director for the Electronic

Frontier Foundation, was quoted in a 2018 CNET article on Dark Caracal and the future of such sucker-punch attacks: "Getting a look into someone's personal device is tremendously personal, it's like getting a look into their mind."[4]

I'd rather that no one took a peek into my mind, how about you? But it's not only during our waking hours that our smartphones may be tracking us. Hidden app trackers, numbering in the thousands, may be pilfering your data from the moment your head hits the pillow tonight. Geoffrey A. Fowler, in an article for *The Washington Post*, writes:

> It's 3 am. Do you know what your iPhone is doing? Mine has been alarmingly busy. Even though the screen is off and I'm snoring, apps are beaming out lots of information about me to companies I've never heard of.[5]

Funny how Fowler's phone conveniently forgot to notify him about all that witching hour secrecy. Other smart devices, including personal voice assistants, are spying on us in similar ways.[6] You might say that your life is an open book and you have nothing to hide, so this data mining doesn't concern you. But if you've checked your bank account information just once on your smart device, then your most valuable data could be at risk.

Even when you're dreaming, data mining companies are collecting "cookies," those tasty tidbits of information about your search history and buying preferences that they sell to the highest bidder. You can run but you can't hide when you're online, even if you're browsing in private mode. Yes, that's right. Norton AntiVirus has been protecting our computers since 1991 and a candid article on the company's website dispels the myth of private browsing. The article asserts how your information may not be stored on any particular device in private mode but may still be accessible to your Internet service provider, the websites you visited, government agencies, and your employer if you did the browsing at work.[7]

Being online is like standing in the middle of Grand Central Station. Eyes and ears are at every turn. Sure, it may feel like you're anonymous, but you always have to be on guard. That odd fellow by the newsstand might be harboring a virus and that smirking gal in the café might want to hack into your briefcase. Who can you trust? Like the pulse point of a megacity, the Internet is a lonely but perilous place. And if you live in one of the new designer smart homes, the risk for hacking is even more consequential. Signing up for a smart home is like scattering a set of spare keys across a high-crime neighborhood. Eventually, a hacker might find that key (or code) to unlock your home without the need for forced entry.

This knowledge, along with Michael Valeri's class, "Swipeless in Seattle: How to Live without a Smartphone," might make you feel better about not having any new notifications. In his seminar-style course, Valeri makes the argument that it is possible and fulfilling to exchange your smart device for a basic phone. If a young technology professional like Valeri is surviving and thriving without little love nudges from Twitter and Facebook every day, then why can't we all?

Some of us crave those new notifications or depend on them despite the privacy invasion. For one person, a new notification may represent the excitement of seeing who has engaged with an online post; for another person the flashing words on the screen can precipitate stress and anxiety. Is that the boss again? What does my mother-in-law want now? Did I really sign up to get a code red alert every time a few raindrops fall?

A daylong barrage of notifications followed by an evening of more of the same leaves us with no time to relax. Each seemingly harmless notification is akin to someone pinching our forearm a little too hard or stepping on our toes as we try to walk by. Turning off notifications is an option, and one that will be explored further in the Offline Rebel Three-Week Action Plan at the end of this book, but what if you could permanently disable those little pinches?

Offline Solution #6: *Imagine your day completely free of electronic notifications. What does it look like from start to finish? Find out by turning off all but your most urgent notifications for an entire day.*

YOU MIGHT REALIZE that you don't always need to be reachable and, more significantly, that you don't always want to be. Recently I was shopping at Publix, the South's signature grocery store known for its fabulous daily BOGO (buy one, get one) deals and feeble cellular signal. As I was walking into the store, I overheard a harried looking woman seething into her smartphone receiver, "I can't hear you! Do you want iced tea or not?!" She may have been conversing with a spoiled child, or perhaps a high maintenance spouse. I'm not sure who was responsible for turning her into a flame-breathing dragon, but I know *what* was responsible. If she had left her phone in the car, or better yet at home, she wouldn't have been engaged in that frustrating exchange. It wasn't an emergency whether she bought iced tea or not, yet she was treating it like a four-alarm fire.

Then there was the man in the produce aisle of Trader Joe's who swore when his phone rang and then gritted a furious greeting, "You're killin' me!" Clearly, people do not like to be bothered when they're grocery shopping. The question is *why* was this caller persisting to nag him even though he was out running an errand? In this case there could have been an urgent matter, or it could have been yet another instance of cell phones conditioning people to expect instant gratification.

Step into Stillness

My apartment complex is a 100 percent smoke-free property and I often see residents stooped on the curb near the exit, cigarette in one hand and smartphone in the other. They look anything but relaxed, crouched down near a busy intersection as exhaust fumes blow in their faces. Perhaps in their minds this cigarette break is a respite, but it's a flimsy excuse for the kind of refreshment that our bodies and minds really need. As Mari Colham writes in her *Medium* article, "Why It's Important to Take a Break from Smartphones and Social Media":

> Quietness, stillness, and meditation allow us to examine our lives and reflect. However, genuine reflection requires taking a break from technology to silence the notifications and monitors.[8]

The stillness that Colham is proposing may be uncomfortable if we use peripheral noise to silence our thoughts. Sitting with our thoughts in silence forces us to peel back layers that we might not want to expose. The smartphone provides a buffer whether we're in public or in solitude. In public, the phone can make us appear busy or important while acting as an intentional barrier to ward off social overtures. In solitude, the phone acts as a different kind of barrier, separating us from ourselves. Perhaps we seek distance from our most troubling thoughts or, more paradoxically, our deepest desires so that we are never disappointed. Smartphones may seem to be a neutral zone, a safe place where nothing extraordinarily good or bad will happen. But if our phones are on, we are also on without a much needed pause.

Adherents to monotheistic religions observe a day of Sabbath, but there is no designated day of rest from technology unless we take the initiative. Smartphones will not power themselves down; the Internet will never stop ticking. More than 95 million posts are shared on Instagram every day. Sixteen million text messages are sent every *minute*. Five new Facebook profiles are created every **second**.[9] I don't know about you, but I'd like to step off that whirling carousel before I get sick.

We need to establish boundaries with our phones as we would do in any other area of our lives. We do not have to be inextricably linked to our devices and their robotic output. The next time someone asks you if you have the "bandwidth" to complete a project, just shrug and tell them that you don't know what they mean. We are humans not avatars and *we* don't need to unplug *ourselves*, but we do need to unplug our gadgets. We don't "recharge" like a battery but we refresh like a fountain. Our spirits and minds require renewal and it is up to us to honor that need.

The Nonstop Work Week

When does your work week begin? If you have a nine to five schedule (which is closer to eight to six these days) then your work week should in theory start on Monday morning. Not so, according to an article in the *Wall Street Journal* that declares Sunday night to be the new Monday morning.[10]

Dubbed the "Sunday Scaries," the last precious few hours of the weekend are frequently lost wading through an overflowing inbox in an effort to jumpstart the work week. Backlash and burnout among employees have led some employers to ban sending emails on the weekends.

But if you use a little program called Slack, then you may not be able to cut yourself any. In an article titled, "Slack Is Ruining My Life and I Love It," CNN business correspondent Seth Fiegerman depicts the communication app as a continuous distraction. Fiegerman writes:

> At any given moment, day or night, when I open the Slack app I am almost guaranteed to see little red dots next to the names of various channels and users telling me how many unread mentions and messages are waiting for me...The casual nature of Slack makes it easier for colleagues and managers to send you messages after work hours...[11]

I can easily see how Slack can ruin someone's life, but I must have missed the part about why that's worthy of love. Perhaps the article title was meant to be ironic, but with more than 10 million users, Slack is "ruining" a whole lot of lives. In fact, Slack was a deal breaker for me in what could have been a part-time remote writing position, the kind that matches 401K contributions and makes hungry freelancers clamor to line up out the door. The company's onboarding process included a staggering ten programs for which individual sign-in credentials were mandatory and each password needed to be unique. As annoying as that rigmarole seemed, I would have gone through it for a chance at a viable retirement savings profile. The clincher, though, was an invitation to join Slack, which I only knew of through the CNN article at the time, so my impression was already less than favorable.

Still, I gave Slack a chance, creating a login with my laptop computer and managing to bypass a memory-draining download of the desktop app. My initial assessment of the busy interface was that it seemed like another social media site where, instead of arrogant selfies, co-workers share pictures of office party birthday cakes, the water cooler shot from a creative angle, and interior decorating ideas for their cubicles. I grinned as I signed off after a few minutes, sensing that I would not become a Slacker. Moments later, when I saw an email from the hiring company requesting that I connect my personal computer to their private network, I knew with certainty that I would have to let go of the pipe dream of matching 401K. Why would I allow a company's IT department to keep a hawk eye on every keystroke I made on my own computer? Like slumbering smartphone users, I would be under constant surveillance. My Rage Against the Machine mentality came swooping back as I penned a letter to human resources and explained that the position would not be a good fit.

However, I do realize that Slack was not designed to be yet another online social forum. The purpose of Slack is to facilitate seamless collaboration among staff members who may all work from one location or who may be spread out across the country and world. So, rather than sending a mass email and making the accidental *faux pas* of CC'ing everyone when BCC'ing is the proper etiquette, you can deliberately spam all your co-workers three feet away and three thousand miles away with a vapid post on Slack. Even after I submitted my resignation I was still bombarded with Slack notifications sent to my email address. Poor punctuation, smiley faces, and terse one-line messages characterized the exchanges I observed before I unsubscribed myself from the group and heaved a sigh of relief.

Slack is only one app, though, among many (and countless more yet to be developed) that intrudes on the well-deserved "free" time of hardworking employees. If ever there was an area that screamed for rebellion, this is it. Imagine if no one from work could reach you on the weekends and when you clocked out on Friday evening the next forty-eight hours plus were all yours. What would you do differently on the weekends if you knew that no colleague or boss could penetrate your sphere of freedom? Technically, we are working for a paycheck, but money is merely the stepping stone and ultimately it is freedom that we hope to gain.

> **Offline Solution #7:** *Do you check your work messages during your off hours? Would it compromise your job if you didn't check them? How can you reclaim your free time to make it yours and not give one crumb of it to your boss? If you've been starting your work week on Sunday night, try shutting the phone down until Monday morning. Doing so might make you feel anxious about what you're missing and fretting about what notifications would pop up on the screen if you powered up the phone. But it will be easier to disconnect the more you practice this self-protective strategy.*

IF YOU WORK in a 24/7 industry, like journalism, then you might not be able to complete this exercise. Somehow I can't picture Anderson Cooper tossing his phone into a dark cellar on Sunday night. But if you don't work for the world's first nonstop news station, then you might consider putting your feet up on the couch during Sunday twilight and reconnecting with your boss and colleagues after the sun rises. You'll wake up feeling more refreshed and equipped to conquer the week and whatever challenges it brings.

New Beginnings

How we begin the day often sets the tone for how the evening will end. If we are frazzled and chaotic from the moment our eyes flutter open, then our days will probably follow the same pattern. We learned in elementary school that a healthy breakfast fuels our entire day yet we don't always adhere to this golden rule. I certainly didn't prior to my smartphone boycott. Here's what a typical morning looked like for me before:

- Wake up late and immediately reach for phone
- Abuse my eyes and groggily scroll for at least half an hour
- Forget that I have a patio and keep my apartment vacuum-sealed
- Feed the aggravated cat scratching my legs and throw together a sugar-laden breakfast (such as chocolate chip granola bars)
- Don't bother to exercise. I'm too tired for that.
- Shower and dress
- Return to my phone for more useless surfing
- Start my work day with a dull headache from screen time lethargy and a bombardment of information I didn't need to know

BUT HERE'S *what a typical morning looks like for me now:*

- Wake up naturally at 6:30 am
- Feed the cat who is delighted that I'm up at sunrise
- Open the door to my patio to breathe in fresh air

- Make a healthy brain food breakfast, like Greek yogurt with mixed berries, and eat it on the patio
- Lace up my sneakers and take a thirty-minute walk around the lake at my apartment complex
- Come back inside, shower and dress
- Read a passage from an inspirational book

BY THIS TIME, the first ninety minutes of the morning have melted away like sweet fondue without my checking anything but the weather by gazing at the sky. By 8 am, I'm ready to turn on the computer and start working if it's a weekday. If it's a weekend, I might not turn the computer on until 10 am – or at all.

The before-and-after transformation symbolizes a stark difference in how I greet each day. Instead of treating my mornings like new beginnings, I used to slip into the zombie-like role that we all play when we allow our phones to maneuver the majority of our waking moments. My inner Wilma Flintstone was not happy and neither was I. If you're displeased with how you start your days, you can take action and flip the control switch so that you're the one with the power – not your device.

For example, I have a friend who used to wake up early so she could catch up on Facebook before dashing to the train station to get to her job as an administrative assistant in Chicago. Exhausted by 10 am, Kate realized that her morning ritual was zapping her of energy before the work day even started. I suggested that she not look at her phone until she's on the train. Reluctantly, she tried my advice. Now, Kate still wakes up about twenty minutes early but to meditate in the living room before facing her urban commute.

Offline Solution #8: *Strategize your mornings with the same* *effort you would give to a major work project. Fill any free time you have with something constructive (meditation) instead of destructive (scrolling). What minor adjustments can you make to balance the beginning of your day? What would your ideal morning ritual be?*

Going Bananas

WE HAVE SEEN how notifications threaten both our privacy and peace. So, if you want to permanently disable those disruptive announcements, then Nokia may have a solution. The retro brand, now owned by Finnish company HMD Global, has reissued its "banana phone" that Keanu Reeves sported in *The Matrix* in 1999. The Nokia 8110 made a bright yellow splash on the market once again in 2018 with an affordable average price tag of $97 across global markets.[12] While the reissued device does provide data access, it does not have a touchscreen. The device's sliding design stretches the phone out like taffy while the uncomplicated interface appeals to nostalgic customers. HMD Global CPO Juho Sarvikas told TechCrunch that "there is a huge population of feature phone loyalists."[13]

To appease these loyalists, the brand reintroduced another classic feature phone, the Nokia 3310, which is even less expensive (as low as $49) and more basic than the banana phone. This reincarnated model sold an eyebrow-raising 70 million units in 2017, proving that there are many of us out there who yearn for the soothing words, "you have no new notifications."

4

BOOKS & BLURBS

"A book has got smell. A new book smells great. An old
book smells even better. An old book smells like ancient
Egypt."
- Ray Bradbury

BROWN SPLOTCHES of age mar the cover and yellow streaks
taint the fading pages. Peeling Scotch tape holds the binding
precariously together and the book feels like it could crumble
in my hands. The inside cover bears a library stamp with a
date of March 29, 1985. All those moons ago my mother
purchased this hardcover edition of *The Little Red Hen* for me
at a library book sale. Even though the book has just about
disintegrated, I have saved it. I have moved twenty-three
times since I was a teenager and this tattered book has
endured through every packing session.

Why have I kept this book for more than thirty years?
Sentimentality is an obvious guess, but I didn't save any of my

Barbie dolls, Milton Bradley board games, Lincoln Logs, or other nostalgic toys I once loved. A few old books, diaries and writing assignments are all that remain as tangible proof of my childhood. Perhaps these specific keepsakes remain because books tell stories that are figurative and literal. Old books are anachronistic yet they are timeless. All books are friends and companions.

My love affair with books may have first flamed on a frigid January morning in the Northeast when I was six days old. As a newborn winter baby, I had only seen the inside of a hospital and my parents' suburban house. But that changed when my mother enshrouded me in blankets thick enough to melt a glacier and drove me to our town's public library for my first official outing. Of course, I remember nothing about this excursion other than my mother's frequent retelling of it, but I like to think that it set the tone for an enduring appreciation of the written word.

During my childhood in the 1980's, the affair blossomed as I learned the science of searching for books in a card catalog. I delighted in pulling open the mahogany drawers and flipping through the seemingly endless index cards. Dewey Decimal was a friend of mine, though I don't know where he is now. (I really hope he's not on Facebook.) Librarians were as familiar to me as my school teachers. My face brightened every time Mrs. D'Angelo handed me a stack of freshly stamped books to tuck away in my backpack. At home, I would examine the previous stamps and count how many years ago the books had been borrowed while imagining where the readers were. Years later, in college, I felt like I had hit the nerd's jackpot when I was assigned to a dormitory across the street from a multi-level Barnes & Noble bookstore.

Libraries and bookstores are still a second home to me. As for those card catalog treasure chests, the infinite searching capabilities of the computer have rendered them defunct, but there is at least one left standing in a small town in Rockland County, New York. The employees at the Pearl River Library maintain a card catalog in the children's section, perhaps as a history lesson or a sort of museum display. Maybe one day that card catalog will stand alongside an incomplete skeleton of some ill-fated Tyrannosaurus Rex. It is my sincerest hope that the book in its glorious physical form will never make it to the museum.

I am not alone in my preference for books that engage the senses. Dr. Bassam Frangieh is a former professor of Arabic at Yale University and currently teaches at Claremont McKenna College in California. Frangieh moved to the United States from Syria in his late twenties and learned not only a new language but also a foreign alphabet during these young adult years. Writing a book in one's native language is a formidable challenge, but the challenge doubles when writing in a second language and perhaps triples when composing in a foreign alphabet. Frangieh has risen to these challenges many times, most recently with his 2018 book, *An Introduction to Modern Arab Culture*.

In a phone interview, Frangieh shared how he conducts his research exclusively through hard copies of books. Though he owns an iPhone and can easily connect to the Internet from anywhere, he chooses to use physical textbooks and dictionaries when completing a writing project.

Frangieh was blunt: "To be honest, I hate these smartphones. They are a major distraction and the only way I can accomplish my research is to turn the device off. I also find it easier to flip through the pages of a book, combing through the table of contents and index, rather than scrolling down a screen. If the screen freezes or the battery gets low, my research gets interrupted. If the mouse doesn't work, again my research stalls. Books don't have that problem."

Further, studies have proven that there is a measurable difference between how our brains process information from a screen and from the pages of a book, newspaper, or magazine. For one, reading a book, with its glossy cover art and smooth pages, is a more aesthetically pleasing experience than scanning the abrasive screen of an e-reader.

Naomi Baron, professor of linguistics at American University in Washington, DC, explains this phenomenon in her article for the *New Republic*, titled "Why Digital Reading Is No Substitute for Print." Between 2013 and 2015, Baron studied the reading habits of more than four hundred university students around the world, from countries as diverse as Slovenia and Japan.

According to Baron, the students in her study made remarks such as "I like the smell of paper" and reading in print form is "real reading." Baron continues in her article: "What's more, print gave them a sense of where they were in the book – they could 'see' and 'feel' where they were in the text."[1]

Additionally, some students in Baron's study expressed how reading digitally was uncomfortable and made their eyes burn. Anyone who has spent more than an hour or so in front of a small mobile device has likely endured that stinging sensation. Even reading on a desktop computer screen can have the same effect. We take breaks from our computers, standing up and stretching every once in a while, but do we step away from the smartphones? I viewed my smartphone as an extension of my leisure time, so I didn't feel the need to take a break. Consequently, my vision suffered and I needed a higher prescription for glasses less than a year after I leased my first smartphone. The American Optometric Association warns that Computer Vision Syndrome (alternately called Digital Eye Strain) is very real and can be either temporary or permanent depending on how we alter our behaviors.[2] While

I haven't been able to revert to a weaker eyeglass prescription, my eyes don't burn after I've spent a few hours with a hardback novel.

Handheld devices like smartphones, tablets, and e-readers are probably worse for our vision than computers. The most obvious reason is because handheld devices have smaller screens than computers, but there are other factors. Because we hold the devices closer to our eyes, the strain is greater, whereas we maintain a safer distance in front of a computer. E-reader devotees might argue that their devices utilize e-ink which is as close to printed words as currently possible. Because it mimics printed words, e-ink is thought to be gentler on the eyes. In addition, new e-reader models claim to be glare-free and feature adjustable warm lights which are not as harsh as the typical blue lights.

E-reader fans could also argue that we hold physical books close to our eyes as well, but we're looking at printed pages versus a screen, glare-free or otherwise. The fact remains that humans have only been reading from screens for a fraction of a percentage of history. For five thousand years, humans read through other means such as the clay tablets of the Fertile Crescent in the ancient Middle East. I wonder what the Mesopotamians and Egyptians would think of what we refer to as "tablets" today.

Then of course there are the distractions that Frangieh overcomes by silencing his smartphone during intense research. Sixty-seven percent of the students in Baron's study claimed they were likely to multitask while reading via a screen, as compared to 41 percent whose attention would be scattered while reading offline.[3] More attempts at multitasking lead to less learning, meaning that it may be both more enjoyable and more effective to read books in their tangible form.

But what about the environmental impact of paperback

and hardcover books? The publishing industry has never been known to be particularly kind to trees. However, that may be changing as some publishers, like mega giant Penguin Random House, have begun printing books with recycled fiber. Further, we can purchase used books, borrow titles from the library, or exchange our favorite reads with family and friends to lessen the environmental impact.

The Joy of Reading

As a voracious reader since childhood, I wish for today's generation and all future generations to know the joys of reading. As a young reader, I cried about the tender friendship between Wilbur the pig and the eponymous spider in *Charlotte's Web*. Reading *Little House in the Big Woods* made me want to abandon my suburban town and befriend a deer in a faraway forest. *Peanuts* comic books made me root for the underdog and feel compassion for outcasts like Charlie Brown.

Great books ignite emotions and children will not soon forget their adventures in reading. The books children read have the power to shape their minds and even their dreams. Beverly Cleary's *Ramona* series whispered to me that I could write my own stories someday. My favorite books are a part of my DNA, a link to my childhood, and a foundation for lifelong learning.

Offline Solution #9: *What are some of the books that wrote the script of your childhood? Do you still have any of them? Would you rather have a hard copy or digital copy of your favorite book from the past? Go to the library and track down a dog-eared copy of your favorite childhood book. Reread the book with fresh eyes and, if there's a child in your life, share the book with him or her.*

Quality or Quantity

UNLESS YOU'RE one of the rare bibliophiles who has built floor-to-ceiling bookshelves in your home, then you probably don't have five thousand physical books at your fingertips. With e-book libraries it is much easier, and cheaper, to accumulate hundreds or thousands of books depending on how many Gigabytes of storage you have. Unfortunately, quantity often comes at the expense of quality in the ballooning e-book market. "Books" of half a dozen pages are routinely published on e-book sales channels. Many of these "books" are riddled with spelling, grammatical and formatting errors that would drive any English professor to raving madness.

Even if you download classic literature on your e-reader, does it elicit the same reaction as it would if you were to hold, feel and yes, *smell* the book up close? Reading is a sensory experience that involves more than the eyes. Walt Whitman's sensual poetry would read very differently by the light of a lemongrass aromatherapy candle than it would on the grubby, fingerprint-smeared screen of an e-reader. Jon Krakauer's *Into Thin Air*, a memoir of climbing Mount Everest before a deadly storm erupts, would probably be riveting in any form. But how much more so if we turn the pages one by one, actively participating in the ascent towards the summit, rather than passively tapping and swiping?

Smartphones, once again, dole out minimal rewards with minimal effort. We do not learn as much through digital reading, nor do we feel as much. Throw in the diagnosis of Computer Vision Syndrome and we'll be writing ourselves prescriptions for the latest paperback.

The eyes are not the only part of our anatomy that screen

reading impacts. Writer's cramp is painless compared to smartphone user's agony that radiates from the dominant hand all the way up to the shoulder, often straining the neck as well. I recall waking up many nights unable to bend my right arm because the pain in my elbow crease was so intense. But this pain became a fading memory once I got rid of my smartphone. Paradoxically, I have cradled a much heavier hardcover book in my arms for hours while reading in bed and have never dealt with any related pain.

Bubble-Headed Blurbs

What about short bursts of digital reading that have nothing to do with books? Much of the reading we do online involves blurbs – bite size snippets of information, gossip and speculation. Our e-readers can hold thousands of books, but the Internet's offerings are limitless. Endless streams of poorly written words and sensationalized news stories bombard our brains and eyes in minute-by-minute blows. Why do we need to know about a personal tragedy that occurred six thousand miles away? Moreover, why does a ten-year-old child need to know? Real tragedies unfold every day in our own lives when the Internet callously strips away the innocence of children.

I saw little of the news as a child, unless you count the upbeat *Good Day, New York* morning show that sent me off to school with a goofy smile on my face. My parents would tune in to the news in the evenings, usually just for half an hour. We didn't have cable, so we were stuck with the handful of local stations that went dark after the last ThighMaster infomercial ended at 2 or 3 am. One late night as a teenager, I flipped on the television set and couldn't find anything to watch but silver fuzz because the stations were sleeping. So, I went back to bed and got enough rest for the algebra quiz I had the next day. In retrospect, I understand how sometimes it is better not to have an excess of options.

Sundays in my household were slow and civilized. The Sunday paper was a family tradition, but we spent as much time on the classifieds and comics (Hello again, Charlie Brown and Snoopy!) as we did on front page headlines. For breakfast, my mother would treat us to jelly doughnuts and carrot cake from the bakery down the street. In mid-afternoon, we would head over to my grandparents' apartment for our weekly family dinner where no one would have dared turn on the television. My uncles told corny jokes while we gorged on spaghetti with homemade tomato sauce and sipped red wine (Ginger Ale for me). Afternoon flowed into evening as we stuffed ourselves with pound cake à la mode and danced to my grandfather's Django records. We were carefree not overburdened, we didn't reside on a roller coaster of emotions throughout the day, waiting for the next atrocity to be announced in blaring red letters.

Fast forward to where we are now with one in ten adults checking the news every hour and one-fifth of adults admitting that they "constantly" monitor their social media feeds.[5] Before smartphones, I had a boyfriend who began each day, including Sundays, with 1010 WINS, a New York area AM radio news station. Because the news was making him depressed, I tried to persuade him that he should work out or read in the morning instead, but he was married to 1010 WINS. We haven't been a couple in years, but I'd bet that his mornings still begin in much the same way, except on his phone rather than on the radio.

Offline Solution #10: *If the homepage on your device is set to an Internet news channel, reset it to a website that makes you smile. There are educational websites that greet you with a word of the* *day and entertainment sites that tell you a daily joke. Once you've reset your homepage, try checking the news less frequently – perhaps just once in the morning and once in the evening.*

YOU MIGHT BE WONDERING: is it really that bad to consume so much news? Readers of *Time* magazine asked that question in 2018 and the publication answered that it might be. The article proclaimed that "staying aware and informed is a good thing. But when it comes to your health, too much news spells trouble."[4] Loretta Breuning, author of the book *Habits of a Happy Brain*, was interviewed in the article and recommended reserving one short block of time each day to check the news (the way we did in the olden days). She also called into doubt the idea that staying in the loop is wise:

> There's this idea of following the news in order to be an informed citizen, but a lot of what you see today is gossip elevated to a sophisticated level.[5]

Gossip disguises itself as news in many forms such as political dirt, celebrity drama, and stories so bizarre that they would shock the editors of the *Guinness Book of World Records*. How much do we actually learn from these dozen word blurbs of lurid gossip anyway? The media's selective sound bites of misinformation have contributed to the polarizing of political views in the United States. Conservative, liberal, or anywhere in between, we can read a controversial headline and immediately become enraged without knowing any of the facts. Don Henley was perceptive in 1982 when he sang "Dirty Laundry" about making an unethical living off the evening news.

Henley's ideas have undergone a 21st century makeover

with the medium of the Internet, but they're more valid than ever. What is the antidote to the discouraging, overhyped, wildly inaccurate news? Disabling news notifications would be a helpful first step. Picking up a paper version of a reputable newspaper could be another step. Getting happily lost in a book on current events – or on just about anything – might be the ultimate medicine for the mind.

CONNECT THE DOTS

**"I'm uninterested in superheroes. I am only interested in
real stories, real people, real connection."
- Jamie Lee Curtis**

MIREILLE GUILIANO, author of the international bestselling
lifestyle guide *French Women Don't Get Fat*, knows a thing or
two about healthy living. She also knew about the
interference of mobile devices in our social lives before the
iPhone even launched. Her follow-up guide, *French Women for
All Seasons*, was published in 2006, one year before Steve Jobs
announced that his invention was on the verge of making
history.[1] In the book, Guiliano paints a sublime picture of her
summer home in Provence, rhapsodizing about the lavender,
the crickets and the sunsets. She also talks about her frequent
houseguests, all of whom were required to leave their early
21st century flip phones at the door:

My only demand is that they surrender all handheld devices – at least telephonic ones – when they cross our threshold. Some city friends really have a hard time and truly don't know how to relax. But once the mind is engaged, once we call our attention to this little wonder and that small miracle, the spirit follows.[2]

Giuliano recognized how technology interrupts our ability to be with others and to benefit from our surroundings. Her depiction of Provence swells with *joie de vivre* and the kind of simplicity that comes from inhaling the perfume of a field of lavender, listening with awe to a chorus of crickets, and staring at an electrifying sunset with someone special at your side. You can do these things with your phone in your hand, but will you truly enjoy them? Some young people don't know any other way.

Adolescent Addicts

Jared was at a sweet sixteen birthday party with a group of peers, none of whom had anything to say to one another. The roomful of teenagers stood around frowning awkwardly at their sneakers or roving their eyes away from each other. Then, one quick-thinking girl whipped out her phone and normalcy automatically resumed. The students had no trouble "communicating" under the camouflage of their screened devices but could not manage to say anything while looking each other in the eye. Granted, adolescence is a time of shyness and developing egos, but this situation is one that could not have occurred at any previous point in history.

The kids did that night what people of all ages tend to do: travel the path of least resistance. Rather than battle with the awkwardness for a few minutes, the kids ran to the nearest emergency exit. I wonder how the party might have been different if any of the youngsters had been brave enough to surmount peer pressure and say, "Come on guys, we don't need our phones, that's lame!"

I was a high school English teacher before I ripped the parachute off and jumped into the storm cloud of freelance writing. In 2014, one of my sixteen-year-old students relayed that sad but all too common story and it still haunts me. Jared seemed embarrassed when he recounted the incident to our class and I surmised that he wished he had been the trailblazer to vanquish the palpable peer pressure filling the room. When I asked him if he enjoyed the party, he shrugged and shook his head. Then I asked him what he ate at the party, what the cake was made from and if coffee was served. Jared not only couldn't remember the flavor of the cake but he also couldn't remember if there had even *been* cake. For all he knew, there might have been giant cupcakes made out of grape chewing gum because he, like his circle of peers, had been too absorbed with their phones to notice.

Many college students are interacting with their phones in the same way as Jared and his high school friends. One study found that undergraduates would choose their smartphones over food. Researchers at the University of Buffalo labelled food and phones as off-limits for a few hours to a group of seventy-six students aged eighteen to twenty-two. At the end of the window of deprivation, students could opt to earn points towards eating a snack or using their smartphones. For most students, smartphones proved to be the greater motivator. Clinical psychology doctoral student Sara O'Donnell led the study and concluded:

> Research is just beginning to investigate the possibility that smartphone addiction exists. While reinforcing value does not equate to addiction, it seems likely that if smartphone addiction becomes a valid diagnosis, those individuals would

have high smartphone reinforcement, just as individuals with alcohol use disorders have high alcohol reinforcement.[3]

Hope for the Future

The much needed bright side is that not all young people are addicted to technology and some even shun it. Take for example my former co-workers Bryson who is twenty years old and his brother Lionel who is twenty-two. They moved to Florida from their native Kansas City, Missouri, and our paths crossed when we worked together as part-timers at a gourmet oil and vinegar shop. An aspiring chef, Lionel was there for the culinary experience; an aspiring writer, I was there for the steady paycheck. Both young men owned Androids but neither spent much time on them and never in front of customers. Buoyed by their openness, I enjoyed many deep, thought-provoking conversations with the brothers about poetry, art and music.

With his straggly auburn hair and shaggy beard, Bryson is a deadringer for the lead singer of Lynyrd Skynyrd – and one day I told him so. To my surprise, he not only knew of the classic rock band from Alabama but was also a diehard fan. Maybe there's no correlation, but I recall mentioning Bruce Springsteen to my smartphone-obsessed twenty-year-old colleague and her face was a blank canvas that would have made Picasso cringe. (Originally from New Jersey, I'm obligated to feel that it's a sacrilege to be uninitiated into King Springsteen's songbook.) Still, I believe that Bryson and Lionel are conversant about a wider variety of topics because they actually *talk* to people and don't hover over their phones at every turn.

When I asked Lionel why he rarely checked his phone, he

told me: "Because it's boring. I don't care what my friends ate for breakfast or how many pictures of themselves they can store on their camera rolls." I wanted to hug him, but I just smiled and nodded.

Jared from the mute birthday party is now about Lionel's age; the two young men are peers who grew up in the same techno-infused era yet they could not be more different. One is terrified of live interaction while the other one seeks it out. One has difficulty making eye contact while the other will stare you down unblinking. I don't know much about either's childhood, so I can only conjecture if their upbringing played a role. I did, however, meet Bryson and Lionel's mother once when she came into our store to buy a jar of pesto sauce. She was warm and open and didn't glance at her phone once. I couldn't help but connect her beaming personality to the exceptional young men she had raised. Regardless, the optimistic takeaway is that some young people are shattering the mold and choosing people over products.

Therefore, we cannot ascribe digital addiction to any one generation. The only difference between Generation Z and all other living generations is that they were raised with the technologies that older cohorts were not. Unless scientists pinpoint a technology-immune gene, then we are all equally susceptible to this addiction. I have observed women in their seventies updating their dating profiles while standing in line at department stores. I have known people of all ages who are the epitome of rudeness as they insist on keeping their phones at arm's length in every social situation. Therefore, unless there is a valid study offering evidence, we cannot make blanket statements about an entire generation's smartphone usage. To every rule, there is an exception.

Besides, wasn't it a Baby Boomer who invented the smartphone? And I'm not talking about Steve Jobs, although he was a Baby Boomer as well. Frank Canova was born in

1956 and is credited with creating the prototype of the smartphone. In 1992, Canova developed the IBM Simon Personal Communicator which enabled users to send emails and facsimiles in addition to placing phone calls. Called IBM Simon for short, the device was bulky and had a brief battery life of one hour. IBM Simon didn't last longer than a couple of years on the market when it was superseded by more sophisticated inventions such as the Palm Pilot and BlackBerry. All of these devices, of course, are now in the annals of technological history while the iPhone gleams as the gold standard of smartphones. History aside, the iPhone, along with its predecessors and successors, has produced deleterious effects on romance for every generation.

Chocolates, Roses & Romance

What could be less romantic than your lover forgetting Valentine's Day? How about your lover sending you an emoji-filled text message to mark the occasion? Romance in the 21st century has been redefined through pixelated symbols including hearts, boxes of chocolates, and my personal favorite (insert sarcasm here) the red rose. While the gesture is "nice" in that harmless, generic way, it cannot compare to the pure romance of receiving a real flower with its scent and texture, its three-dimensional life, and its tangible softness in the palm of your hand, whispering to you that you are loved.

Indeed, what could be *more* romantic than being presented with a fresh flower, eyes locked with those of the giver, on any day of the year? If you imagine the most romantic experience you ever had, it is unlikely that any type of mobile technology was involved. Yet most of us are bringing those romance-killing devices into the most intimate of all places: the bedroom.

My friends, Bella and Derek, have been married for three

years, placing them beyond the honeymoon phase into the nitty gritty, often dull routines of quotidian life. Bella frequently laments to me how much time Derek spends on his smartphone, checking on sports scores and ogling attractive women on social media. Yet she is equally fixated on her own device, beginning and ending each day by checking Instagram and skating through the nearly 1,500 accounts that she follows. In the microcosm of their home life, Bella and Derek are like all of us at the party or on the subway as we choose our smartphones over the people right in front of us: together but alone.

Photographer Eric Pickersgill illustrates this concept in his unsettling monochrome series titled "Removed." One particularly eerie photograph, "Angie and Me," depicts a woman and man lying in the same bed, facing in opposite directions with their eyes fixed on their hands that appear to be holding smartphones. But looking a little closer at the photo, the viewer realizes that an optical illusion is in play: the disconnected couple's hands are shaped to grasp their smartphones, but Pickersgill has edited the devices out of the picture. The result is a spooky commentary on how we can be so close to someone – mere inches away in the same bed – and yet living completely separate lives.

In the "Removed" project statement on his website, Pickersgill writes:

> ...personal devices are shifting behaviors while simultaneously blending into the landscape by taking form as being one with the body. This phantom limb is used as a way of signaling busyness and unapproachability to strangers while existing as an addictive force that promotes the splitting of attention between those who are physically with you and those who are not.[4]

Of his relationship with his wife, Pickersgill adds: "We rest back to back on our sides coddling our small, cold, illuminated devices every night."[5]

In fact, the couple in Pickersgill's photo is none other than the photographer himself and his wife, Angie. Pickersgill was brave to reveal this scene from his domestic life, which has become commonplace across the developed world. But there is a remedy, whether you are one half of a couple or not. Banish your phone from the bedroom.

Creating a Bedroom Sanctuary

Let's tackle what should be the most peaceful space in our homes: the bedroom. As Pickersgill demonstrated, the bedroom has become a place where devices receive more attention than significant others. A shocking 10 percent of people have admitted to checking their phones during the most intimate activity, giving new meaning to the term *coitus interruptus.*[6]

Is your bedroom a peaceful haven where you relax after a hectic day of work and responsibilities? Or does the room feel like a continuum of stress that blurs the lines between your work and leisure time? If you're taking your phone into the bedroom, or even worse, into your actual *bed*, then you're a candidate for a bedroom makeover.

You don't have to go shopping or hire an interior designer for this room renovation. The only thing you really need to do is to outlaw your devices. Your smartphone should not be a fixture in this most sacred of spaces, but neither should your tablets or televisions, in essence anything with a screen. If you like to fall asleep watching the nightly news, playing a few rounds of Bejeweled on your iPad, or binge watching the latest Netflix drama, then this might seem like a radical idea.

But it's not so radical when you consider how non-negotiable sleep is as part of a healthy lifestyle. Plus, it turns out that watching television before bed can have some of the same detrimental effects as gazing at your smartphone. Melatonin secretion slows or stops as the light from the screen (any screen) tricks your body into believing that it's daytime. Your body and brain can experience the same confused reaction if you live in a brightly lit city, but in that case you have the option of hanging black-out curtains to block the light pollution.

With smartphones and other screened devices, we can create an invisible black-out curtain by removing the offending objects before they have the chance to wreak havoc on our sleep. Even if your brain is able to fight the deception that it's daytime and fall unconscious, there's a good chance that your sleep quality may still be compromised, say medical experts.

Dr. Susan Biali Haas has written about the phenomenon of REM, short for rapid eye movement, which represents the deepest layers of slumber we can experience. In her *Psychology Today* article "6 Ways That Night-time Phone Use Destroys Your Sleep," Haas writes:

> REM sleep is a stage of sleep that is critical for restoration of your mind and body. REM sleep solidifies memories and is tied to your creative and problem-solving skills. If you don't get enough of it, it can leave you feeling groggy and having difficulty concentrating the next day.[7]

This lack of good quality sleep not only leads to the morning crankiness Haas describes but also to cravings for junk food, a slower metabolism and, consequently, a higher risk of obesity. Plain and simple, we need our sleep! Cutting the cable on our electronic devices may be the simplest and safest way to soak in more of that coveted REM sleep. It's certainly a healthier alternative to swallowing over-the-counter sleeping pills every night. Instead of going to the pharmacy for a melatonin supplement, we can facilitate our body's natural production of the hormone by turning out all the lights, especially the ones that project from screens.

Top 10 Tips to Create a Relaxing Atmosphere in the Bedroom

1. Keep your phone elsewhere. Period.
2. Convert the room into a screen-free space: no tablets, no televisions, no screens whatsoever, except the ones on your windows.
3. Use a white noise machine that projects sounds of nature like a fire crackling or waves crashing.
4. Use tea light candles, salt lamps, and other soft lighting touches to help your eyes and mind rest.
5. Keep an inspiring book on your nightstand and read one chapter before bed every night.
6. Clear away clutter. Keep medicine bottles in the bathroom vanity rather than on the dresser; fold your clothes and put them away neatly; make your bed before jumping into it.
7. Keep plants in your bedroom, especially those that release cleansing oxygen at night. Most plants release carbon dioxide after dark, but some (like orchids and succulents) give out oxygen and can help you fall asleep.
8. In a journal, write five things that you are grateful for every night before dozing off. The items on your list can be as simple as "the rain stopped just in time for the family picnic" or "this blanket keeps me warm."
9. Decorate your walls with soothing scenes like a photo of a moonlit lake or a snowy cabin in the woods.
10. Welcome little feet and paws into your bed only if they don't jeopardize your sleep.

If there's any media at all in your bedroom, let it be some ethereal music that sends you into a sleep-nourishing trance. The atmospheric rhythms of Vanessa Daou and the vocal richness of Peabo Bryson do the trick for me.

Offline Solution #11: *Select a few artists whose music eases your mind and spirit. Instead of looking at media before bed tonight, listen to one of these artists. Sweet dreams may be a song or two away.*

Finding True Connection

TONY REINKE, in his book *12 Ways Your Phone Is Changing You*, focuses on taming the smartphone beast rather than vanquishing it. He does, however, praise the notion of shedding the device like a second skin:

> Giving up a smartphone is not only one of the bravest and most countercultural acts of defiance possible today, it is a gift to others...To any addict brave enough to go smartphone free, I applaud you. You will serve the people around you in unseen ways that will never be noticed or celebrated."[8]

Our decisions and actions are always more meaningful when they benefit others. Have you considered how losing your smartphone for good could benefit your spouse, your children, your parents and friends, all the people who make up the essential fabric of your life?

After I got rid of my smartphone, I witnessed a vast improvement in how I relate to my loved ones. In face-to-face meetings, I no longer rummaged through my purse to find my phone to send the clear but unintended message that its contents were more important than the person in front of me. I'm embarrassed to admit that I sometimes scrolled through my phone even when engaged (or perhaps disengaged) in a voice conversation. I became a better listener and more attentive friend once the smartphone was out of the picture.

On the other hand, I also became more aware of how my loved ones were depriving us of quality time by giving precedence to their phones. Those frequent beeps, which had once seemed almost normal, now grated on my nerves to the point that I wanted to throw other people's phones off the nearest bridge.

For example, what could have been a romantic getaway to Vermont with a man I was crazy about morphed into a nightmare weekend of incessant notifications. My travel partner, let's call him Boris, kept his phone in his hand from check-in at the mountainside inn to check-out seventy-two hours later. He went to the bathroom and the phone went with him. When too much togetherness grated on his nerves, he turned his back to me and fidgeted with his phone. At dinner he answered his work emails. At breakfast he applied filters to our travel photos. When we watched a true crime show on television, he kept one eye on his phone while nagging me to fill him in about the plot of the program.

"Wait, no, wait, did she just get murdered or is she the murderer?" He asked with a straight face as I looked out the window so he wouldn't see me roll my eyes.

Somehow I conjured the self-control to stop myself from ripping the phone out of his hands and hurling it at the Green Mountains. But I had never felt so lonely in the presence of another person. Boris's phone was a third wheel, a mistress even, and I felt like the unwelcome outsider. I refused to compete for his attention with a technological toy, so I spent the last day of the trip in my own world, basking in the bracing mountain air while Boris missed everything but the notifications on his phone. His relentless disengagement from reality was blatant avoidance stemming from fear of intimacy. After our misadventure in New England, Boris and I parted ways, but I have no doubt that he is still in a serious relationship with his phone.

> **Offline Solution #12:** *The next time you're alone with someone special, promise that person a phone-free evening. You might be surprised at the romance that can unfold when it's permitted to free form. But romance does not only exist between two people in love. We can discover romance in other aspects of our lives, whether we're cuddled inside our favorite armchair reading a book of poetry or sampling a tapas menu at the new Spanish restaurant in town. Romance and sensual experiences find us at every turn when we open our hearts to receiving them.*

OVERALL, though, the changes in my relationships were positive. Some of my associates became more cognizant of how much they were using their devices. One afternoon I was out to lunch with a friend who placed her phone next to her napkin and proceeded to glance at it approximately every forty-five seconds. I've never had much of a poker face, so my strained expression must have communicated to Debbie that I was offended. Finally, when the server brought out our desserts, Debbie put the phone in her purse and made the first real eye contact with me since we had arrived at the restaurant.

"I'm sorry – it's like I'm having lunch with an alien today, or my mother," Debbie faltered, then corrected herself. "No, I think what you're doing is very cool, but I just could never do it. I really am on my phone too much, though. I don't know how to stop." She sighed and stabbed her fork into a slice of pecan pie.

"I'm writing a book about living without a smartphone," I announced before taking a sip of herbal tea.

Debbie's face puckered like a compressed sponge and I wasn't sure if it was from the hyper sweetness of the pie or from my book idea. In the next breath I found out that it was the latter. "Flora, like I said, it's incredible that you're doing this, but no one is going to read that book."

Even total strangers reacted to my countercultural decision. One afternoon I carried my laptop into a UPS store where I needed to print a return label. Ordinarily, I would have flashed the barcode from my smartphone like a smooth operator. The twenty-something man at the register looked quizzically at my clumsy computer and commented that I was the first person to ever bring a laptop into the store. I shared with him how and why I didn't own a smartphone anymore. He did a double take, nodded, and said with a wide eyed grin, "Very respectable." I doubt that this encounter influenced the young man to permanently power down his phone, but I did give him food for thought and that meal could be a triumph for every person in his life.

REARVIEW MIRROR

"Technology can be our best friend, and technology can also be the biggest party pooper of our lives. It interrupts our own story, interrupts our ability to have a thought or daydream, to imagine something wonderful..."
- Steven Spielberg

EXHILARATION WAS in the air as the lights of the auditorium dimmed and a spotlight shone on the stage. The energy was palpable while I settled into my seat and awaited the start of the show. Then, a collective hiss of whispers snaked through the audience as an announcer informed: "Ladies and gentlemen, all photography is prohibited at this evening's performance. Please make sure your cell phones are turned off and refrain from using them for any photos or videos during the show. Now without further ado, Sarah McLachlan!"

I clapped my hands and cheered as the creatress of

"Building a Mystery," "Possession," and countless other cherished songs of my youth graced the stage. Directly behind me, a young woman of about twenty gasped then griped that she wouldn't be able to take any pictures. As the applause died down and Sarah was poised to perform before a mesmerized audience, I heard the young woman whine, "But I have to post pictures of this concert!"

As the woman carried on, I wondered if she had ever considered how performers feel to be blinded by flashing cameras from every direction. Wouldn't the technology be an intrusion for musicians as well as the audience? British singer Adele once expressed her displeasure in the middle of a concert, calling out a would-be amateur photographer as she beseeched, "Can you stop filming me with that video camera? Because I'm really here in real life. You can enjoy it in real life."[1]

I took Adele's prudent advice. Once Sarah sat down at the piano and started singing, I forgot about the indignant concertgoer behind me, but I have never forgotten the bitter words she muttered on her way out of the theatre after the show: "That was pointless."

If the woman's only purpose in attending the concert was to snag a dozen Insta-worthy pictures to share with her five hundred anonymous followers, then I suppose the show was "pointless." But if she had purchased a ticket for the reason I did, to immerse myself in the contemplative lyrics and lilting music of the Grammy winning founder of Lilith Fair, then she would have left electrified. I remember the fine toothed comb details of that evening, from Sarah's stylish ripped jeans to her moving stories about her relationship with her teenage daughters. Sure, I would have loved to have a photo to commemorate the special evening, but the truth is that I'll always have a mental image and it's a sparkling one.

However, I have not always been immune to the

temptation to digitally chronicle the most spectacular moments. A few years ago, I made the mistake of living life in the rearview mirror during a themed yoga retreat, ironically, on the power of the present moment. The exquisitely photogenic island of Aruba proved too enchanting to resist. Throughout my week at the retreat, I had tried in vain to capture an image of the sun in that elusive speck of time when it's dipping past our vision and the sky is a kaleidoscope of fiery colors.

On my last evening in Aruba, smartphone in sweaty hand, I literally *ran* westward on the beach in one more fruitless quest to document the Caribbean sunset. As I walked back to the hotel with slouching shoulders, I noticed two people pointing and laughing at me. Frankly, I couldn't blame them because I had acted like a fool to attempt to seize a moment out of the sky and pack it in my suitcase like a keychain souvenir. I should have savored every second of the tropical sunset, a vision so stunning that I didn't need a photograph to remember it. Sadly, I was so obsessed with getting a digital picture of the natural wonder that I hardly paid any attention to it when it was right before my eyes.

Many of us are trying to grab the best moments of our lives and seal them away in glass jars like fireflies. In doing so, we may be missing out on events and emotions that can never be reproduced. In her book, *The Power of Off: The Mindful Way to Stay Sane in a Virtual World*, author and psychotherapist Nancy Colier writes about her experiences as a parent trapped in the digital realm. Colier discusses a recurring scenario at her daughter's dance studio: every mother and father fiddling with their devices during a performance rather than experiencing the joy firsthand. Colier observes:

I wager we probably miss half our experiences while trying

to figure out how to preserve them. This is because we want to possess our experiences the way we would an object.[2]

But honestly who can blame us? I wanted to hold onto that enchanting sunset forever, just as the parents wanted to relive memories of their children with the tap of a screen, and just as you might want to clutch your most incredible moments. My friend, Natalya, whose son celebrated his third birthday in the spring, wanted to enshrine the occasion so desperately that an accident ensued. A group of ten of us sat down to dinner at a Thai restaurant. Natalya took a picture of every curry puff and bowl of tom yum soup before the ultimate photo-op arose when a candlelit confetti cake arrived at the table. The phone was already in Natalya's hand as she stretched her arm high above the table to get an aerial video of her son blowing out the candles. Somehow, the phone slipped out of her hand and landed squarely on the little boy's head. A screaming tantrum erupted and Natalya's husband berated her for being so careless. The boy had been inches away from flaming candles and the accident could have been horrific. Thankfully, he left with a bump on his head and a cautionary tale for all of us.

Perhaps being more selective about the pictures we take would be the happy medium between refraining and excess. After all, if a picture speaks a thousand words as the adage goes, shouldn't one or two be adequate to communicate the beauty or happiness of a bygone moment? Is a picture still worth a thousand words when there are at least a thousand pictures of ourselves sitting in our camera phone at any given time? In decades past, gazing at a photograph had a sacred quality; in war time, sometimes all transatlantic sweethearts had was one, blurry, cracked, black-and-white image of each other. Such a photograph, along with handwritten letters, would carry lovers through months or even years apart. If the lovers had peered through those camera lenses multiple times a day, the resulting photographs would have lost their preciousness. What is rare or slips through our fingers like pixie dust is perceived as more valuable.

Offline Solution #13: *Select one favorite photo of each of the most special people (and/or pets) in your life. Print out the photos and frame them or keep them in your wallet. Like paperback and hardcover books, physical photographs have an intimacy that is lost behind a screen.*

The Selfie Obsession

THEN THERE ARE ALL the pictures that we insist on capturing of ourselves. Self-photography has become so widespread that Oxford Dictionaries' 2013 word of the year was "selfie."[3] Since the coining of the term, selfies have become more popular and it is astonishing that there are accessories specifically designed to help us photograph ourselves. But is this self-obsession a phenomenon that sprung up in the new millennium?

An archaic form of the selfie stick may have been used as early as 1925 and demonstrates how our collective narcissism is not exclusive to the digital era; we simply have a larger forum through which to express it.[4] The Roaring Twenties edition of the selfie stick was a homemade apparatus which a British man named Arnold Hogg used to capture a photo of him and his bride, Helen. In the photo Hogg grins, grips a cigarette between his lips and extends a pole, the presumed vintage selfie stick, as his wife looks on in bewilderment.

This early 20th century picture, if authentic, proves how

our desire to fawn over ourselves is not a contemporary concept. In addition, many prominent artists in history painted self-portraits, from Paul Gauguin to Frida Kahlo. However, these artists did not paint a hundred self-portraits every day of the year the way many social media users prolifically capture personal images on their phones. An incidental selfie may be acceptable, but if we take constant pictures of ourselves, we are not looking outward at the cosmos or inward towards our spirits. We're simply staring *at* ourselves like Narcissus in that clear, tempting pool of water.

Temptation abounds as we have a much more far-reaching opportunity today to express the innate narcissism of human nature with our numerous social media platforms, not to mention revamped selfie sticks. Today, selfie sticks are available in seductive colors like lipstick pink and ocean blue, as well as a range of lengths so we can produce the illusion that someone else snapped the shot. The modern selfie stick made its debut in 2014 when *Time* magazine named it one of the best inventions of the year, but not everyone is equally impressed with the innovation. In fact, selfie sticks have been banned at numerous tourist attractions, including most Disney and Six Flags theme parks worldwide and the Coachella festival stateside.[5]

In some cases, selfie sticks may have been banned because they're a nuisance, but for other businesses, like Disney, safety is a legitimate concern. Disney's policy change came on the heels of a 2015 incident when a California Screamin' roller coaster was shut down mid-ride for close to an hour after a rider broke the rules and whipped out a selfie stick.[6] The accessories were already banned on rides at the time of the roller coaster debacle, presumably to reduce the risk of riders toppling over while trying to catch a flattering shot. But Disney World swiftly expanded its policy to exclude selfie sticks from any section of their theme parks, including the ever-popular setting of the restroom. (Because what could be more glamorous than a photo with a toilet in the background?) The decision is not surprising when we consider how people have walked off cliffs to their deaths while absorbed in the virtual goings-on of their smartphones, especially the quest for the perfect pixelated self-portrait.

And what about how many pictures some of us are taking (and posting) of our children without their consent? People have amassed thousands of photos of their progeny long before the first baby tooth is cut. Some of the online photos I've glimpsed of my friends' daughters, decked out in cherry lip gloss and posing with their hands on their hips, are nothing less than exploitative. If we as adults want to document our own lives in photos, then we have every right to, but the rules should be modified when it comes to innocent children.

Living without a Smartphone Is Easy

As I took a seat in the swivel chair, the hairstylist was squinting at her phone, pert ginger bob swinging back and forth as she shook her head in consternation. Patricia glanced up from the screen and gave me a sheepish smile. "I'm sorry – just give me one second. My sister-in-law is having a crisis."

Some tense minutes later, Patricia tossed the phone onto her work station like a hot potato and apologized again. "Sometimes I really hate that thing," she said.

"That's why I got rid of mine," I replied quietly as she blinked.

"What are you talking about?" She asked suspiciously as I shared how my life had become easier since I no longer had a mobile phone.

Patricia laughed as she wondered aloud, "But how can you really live without a phone? It's not possible."

"I know of a woman who lived seventeen years without money," I challenged. Now I had her attention.

Heidemarie Schwermer grew up in pre-World War II Prussia. She was the privileged daughter of a wealthy businessman who employed a nanny and gardener, among other household staff. When war broke out in Europe in 1939, Schwermer's family lost everything and fled to Germany. Years later, Schwermer's father rebuilt his empire and founded a tobacco company. Once again the daughter of an affluent man, Schwermer could have had anything she wanted.

Instead, she worked as a teacher and psychotherapist before deciding that an empty wallet, not a sizable bank account, would set her free. In 1994, in her early fifties, Schwermer founded Germany's first exchange circle to connect people to swap services for goods rather than money. A housekeeper, for example, might exchange cleaning services for new clothing in Schwermer's "Give and Take Central" program. As Schwermer became more involved in this endeavor over the next several years, she realized that she didn't need money to live a rich life. Schwermer sold almost all her belongings and packed her few remaining necessities in a suitcase before moving into a friend's home where she had agreed to house-sit for a year.

In 2012, still immersed in her cashless lifestyle, Schwermer told *Business Insider:* "I noticed less and less that I needed money. I didn't want to go back to my old life...I am something like a peace pilgrim. I go from house to house sharing my philosophy."[7]

Echoing my sentiments about living without a phone, Schwermer asserted that giving up money provided her a better quality of life, along with freedom and a more valuable type of wealth. Decades earlier, consumerism had left a bitter taste in her mouth when she visited Chile and witnessed extreme poverty. The year she spent in that South American country propelled Schermer to be steadfast on her quest to live without money until her death.[8]

Though she lacked a permanent address, Schwermer did not consider herself homeless. She perceived herself as more of an earth shaker, shattering the normal and reshaping it into something odd but oddly wonderful. "Now, more and more young people want to change something in their lives and often they don't know what they can change. I changed something in my life."[9]

When Heidemarie Schwermer passed away in Germany in 2016 at the age of seventy-four, she was still holding fast to her principles. She left behind two children and three grandchildren who didn't always agree with her unorthodox choices, but Schwermer's beliefs were too powerful for even her family to dissuade her:

> People are too involved with the material world — money, possessions...They spend tons of time and energy on it. And they aren't aware of how little money actually provides for them! I wanted to prove that another lifestyle is possible.[10]

Because Schwermer lived according to her values, she never looked back in disappointment. Until her final days, she was traveling across Europe, giving lectures, writing books, and innovating ways to subsist without money. Any funds earned from these ventures she handed out to strangers on the street. Schwermer's decision to empty her pocketbook led to a series of events that gave her a modest degree of fame and a unique example of how to stay rooted in the present. Without a credit card, she didn't think about what she might need in the future or sacrifice her future for what she might want now. Without a cash income, she lived moment by moment and never had to worry about whether she would lose her job, get evicted, be a victim of burglary. Some would say that her whole life was tucked into a single suitcase, but I would propose that her life took place everywhere outside that suitcase. Similarly, if you've ever misplaced your phone and panicked, "My whole life is in that phone!" then you might want to broaden your perspective.

After I finished my story, Patricia dabbed some mousse into my hair and chuckled, "Maybe I *could* live without my phone. It's got to be easier than what Heidemarie did!"

> **Offline Solution #14:** *Challenge yourself to live without money for one day, not spending any cash or charging any purchases to your credit cards. If that seems too easy, then try two or three days. If you can live without money for at least a day, then giving up your phone may not be as difficult as you think. After all, you have used money almost your whole life, whereas your smartphone crashed through the door much more recently.*

THIS MORNING, as I was writing this chapter, I got up from my desk to take a break on my patio. The sky was clear, so I was surprised to see a rainbow shining over the blue horizon. My gut reaction was to want to take a picture of it, but I wasn't sure where my digital camera was – and I had just finished extolling the virtues of presence! So, I practiced what I preached by staying rooted to the lawn chair and gazing at the rainbow until it disappeared, which happened barely two minutes later. If I had tried to photograph the image, I would have missed it. The rainbow would have slipped through my restless fingers like the sunset in Aruba. What will you do the next time you bear witness to a majestic sight in nature? I hope you will savor it.

II

CREATE NEW MAGIC

"I must be a mermaid...I have no fear of depths and a great fear of shallow living."
- Anaïs Nin

SCREEN-FREE LIVING SPREE

**"All of our technology is completely unnecessary to a
happy life."**
- Tom Hodgkinson

A WORLD away from the noise and smog of Los Angeles,
Catalina Island is an enviable place to unpack your bags. Deep
blue Pacific waters, abundant wildlife, and palm trees whisper
of paradise. When Marisa's seventh grade class took a trip to
Catalina Island, the students were invited to enjoy everything
this celestial slice of earth has to offer – everything except
technology. For one whole week, these smartphone savvy
teenagers were forbidden from checking or even touching
their devices. Most of the kids groaned at the restriction, but
a few of them were grateful for the opportunity.

Marisa, whom I tutored virtually in writing for two years,
described the tech-free week as "blissful." She told me that she
spent more time in face-to-face conversation with her

classmates than she ever had, even the ones who had initially shunned the technology fast. A novelist in the making, Marisa also started a new writing project on the trip. Filling up notepads with fresh storylines and intriguing characters, Marisa drew inspiration from the cliffs and boats that were foreign to this Texas girl who had never seen the ocean before stepping foot on Catalina Island.

At the end of the trip, everyone turned their phones back on, including the teacher chaperones who had also been digitally abstaining. Marisa relayed to me how her homeroom teacher received a devastating message within a few seconds of powering up her phone. The teacher's boyfriend of three years had broken up with her via text message, knowing that her phone was off and that she would not be able to respond. The cowardice and passive-aggressiveness of that action warrants another whole chapter and even teenage Marisa understood the teacher's distraught reaction. She recalled patting her tear-stricken mentor on the shoulder and saying, "What would a loser like him have done before cell phones?"

On the bus ride to the airport, things largely returned to "normal" and the ink on Marisa's notepads dried out. When she arrived at her home near El Paso, and all the distractions of a digital environment restarted, the freshly hatched writing project fell by the wayside. She admitted that she couldn't concentrate with her friends texting her every few minutes with banal announcements like "just had a burger" and pointless questions such as "r u bored?"

During our twice weekly Skype sessions, I encouraged Marisa to turn her Texas town into Catalina Island for an hour each day and laser focus on her writing. She was receptive to this idea and tried for a while to resume the project, but ultimately the distractions proved too strong.

The irony of our online tutoring was not lost on me and I realized that I was contributing to a problem that I was trying to solve. Marisa's parents had hired me to help their daughter become a better writer, but how could I do that from another time zone, through an impersonal box of glass? I felt guilty for adding two hours a week to her screen time, hours that she could have poured into her abandoned writing project. Or, instead of staying cooped up in the house all day, she could have kicked a soccer ball around outside with her two younger brothers who were always soliciting her attention.

Unable to justify the virtual tutoring, I resigned from my position while writing this book and have ended the web-based business. For several years, online tutoring paid close to half my bills, but I could not be a hypocrite, so I have replaced the income with meatier writing assignments while fielding occasional emails from Marisa and responding with words of motivation about her dreams of becoming a bestselling novelist. Last time I heard from Marisa, she told me that she has a new virtual tutor – and they meet five hours a week.

Online Solution #15A: *Create your own version of Catalina Island by taking a day trip to the most scenic location you can find. Keep all devices silent and pay attention to the sounds and sights around you. What do you notice? Write about or a draw a picture of your personalized Catalina Island and try to keep the devices off until you're back home.*

THE LAST TIME my life resembled Catalina Island was in 1997. I was an American in Paris, newly minted from high school and working as a nanny for five unruly children. In the ritzy Parisian suburb of Meudon, I lived in servant quarters on the attic level of a mansion surrounded by wrought iron gates and gargoyles. Home Internet was still an emerging concept in the late 1990s and my wealthy employers didn't have a connection, though they did have a fax machine for business purposes. I hadn't yet acquired an email address and associated Internet usage with research rather than amusement, so the lack of web access was inconsequential. (Plus, I was too busy combing the streets of Paris for raspberry cream puffs and other decadent French delights to care.) The family of seven also shared one desktop computer which I was not permitted to use. There was no television in my quarters and my only entertainment besides books was a Sony Walkman cassette player.

As a teenager, I didn't appreciate the minimalism because it was normal in that era, but in retrospect I think such a simple arrangement would make a delicious vacation. Millions of other people apparently agree, as digital detox getaways are rising in popularity and availability around the world. The concept is simple: you book a package to an off-the-grid place, like the high desert of northern New Mexico, and you leave everything behind – your devices and your worries. The accommodations are spartan, usually consisting of a bed, desk, chair, and perhaps a recliner.

Some digital detox getaways are more luxurious. For example, Canyon Ranch in Lenox, Massachusetts, boasts a spa and employs a wellness staff comprised of acupuncturists, massage therapists, and sleep experts. The ranch offers a retreat where phones are not forbidden but limited to designated areas of the resort. The staff of Canyon Ranch treats guests to a plethora of activities, from watercolor painting to aerial yoga, in the hopes of keeping those tech-friendly areas empty.

The most restrictive type of digital detox trip is the silent retreat which frowns upon all types of communication, including face to face conversations. One CNBC correspondent took a silent retreat to Bali, Indonesia, where he survived three days without his phone. Uptin Saiidi depicts the experience as challenging in a daily rundown of his trip published on the CNBC website. Saiidi does, however, admit:

> After the retreat, I felt more relaxed and even more present in conversations. But within a few weeks, my phone habits and screen time reverted to where I was before, and I fell back in the habit of too much swiping, liking, and posting.[1]

WHAT SAIIDI CONSIDERS A "HABIT," others call an "addiction," but the fact remains that he was unable to sustain his offline behavior once the phone was in his possession again. This observation may make digital detoxing, at a bare minimum, even more vital since forcing ourselves to unlatch our death grip on those devices is often the only way to be free. But there's no reason to traverse the globe or board a plane to benefit from this freedom. You can orchestrate a relaxing staycation in the comfort of your home.

Offline Solution #15B: *Can you promise yourself (and your loved ones) a day each week when screens are obsolete in your household? Take your Catalina Island experience to the next level and progress from a few hours without your phone to an entire day without any screens. If you did the bedroom sanctuary makeover from Chapter 5, then you might like to coordinate the day and night so that you have a full twenty-four hour respite from technology each week.*

Wisdom from the Greatest Generation

BORN in 1924 at the sunset of the Greatest Generation, my father was approaching his senior years when I was born. Victor never owned a mobile device of any kind, unless you count the walkie talkies that he used to tinker with on Saturday afternoons. With the exception of his favorite classic television sitcoms like *I Love Lucy* and *Fawlty Towers*, my father's entire life was a screen-free living spree. My father never spent one millisecond on the Internet because he didn't use a computer either. Victor spoke French and studied Latin; he could do the most mind-bogglingly advanced calculations in his head, beyond those required in his career as a bank auditor. He was an intellectual, chivalrous version of Fred Flintstone if you can picture such a mash-up. (I guess that would make me Pebbles rather than Wilma.) Until he passed away from Parkinson's disease in 2007, his life was rich and stimulating, filled with thirty-mile bike rides through winding roads in the Catskill Mountains of New York and intellectually rewarding games of chess with friends.

He loved to read and infused the same love in me from the time I could talk. I remember sitting next to him on the sofa with a pile of books taller than I was. One by one, we would open the books and I would describe the colorful scenes on the pages while he listened with infinite patience. Years later when I became a passionate reader, I would ask Dad for book recommendations. One of his finest was Simon Winchester's *The Surgeon of Crowthorne: Murder, Madness and the Oxford English Dictionary*. Who knew that a British reference book would have such an exciting backstory?

My father also had an exceptional attention span, often devoting hours to working on the *New York Times* crossword puzzle and not stopping until every square was filled in with the correct answer. Even with my smartphone phase months in the past, I'm not sure if I would have the same focus and have yet to complete even one of those challenging puzzles. Could it be that it is not merely the smartphone but the entire virtual universe - starting with the World Wide Web - that has irrevocably changed me? Nicholas Carr, author of *The Shallows: What the Internet Is Doing to Our Brains*, believes that it is. In the prologue to his book, Carr writes:

> Media work their magic, or their mischief, on the nervous system itself. Our focus on a medium's content can blind us to these deep effects. We're too busy being dazzled or disturbed by the programming to notice what's going on inside our heads. In the end, we come to pretend that technology itself doesn't matter. It's how we use it that matters, we tell ourselves. The implication, comforting in its hubris, is that we're in control. The technology is just a tool, inert until we pick it up and inert again once we set it aside.[2]

The way Carr frames his argument makes it sound as though technology has already won the battle for dominion over our brains. If he is right, then scrubbing our lives of mobile technology may not undo all the damage, but the bold move of trashing our smartphones appears now not only liberating but also dire. Instead of making our phones inert, we can make them invisible, although they may never be completely irrelevant. Our dependence on digital technology may now be part of our genetic blueprint, an evolution of sorts that will never vanish even after generations.

If we subscribe to Carr's perspective, we can trace this change back to the 20th century rather than consider it a novelty of the new millennium. As a high school student in the mid-1990s, I used a predominance of physical books combined with a smattering of online articles to complete research papers. In retrospect I realize that my brain could already have been going through the changes that Carr depicts in his book.

My sophomore year history teacher delighted in assigning ridiculously long, boring research reports on a weekly basis. One week, my assigned topic was both broad and daunting: the causes of the Revolutionary War. It was a topic that I found less than inspiring, one that had been rehashed in every history lesson I had received since kindergarten. So, instead of reading the appropriate chapter in my history textbook or borrowing a few books from the library, I surfed the Internet for the very first time. The amount of information online was overwhelming and I had trouble assimilating the details. Surfing from one website to the next, bouncing from one thought to another without having fully fleshed out a thesis and supporting ideas, I was on a rocky hike down to The Shallows. This stumble occurred when there were a mere 23,500 websites in 1995 versus the more than one billion up and running in 2019.[3] It is unfathomable how this inexhaustible array of websites must be scrambling our brains today.

For this reason and countless others, I have limited my online time even on my laptop. Passive surfing of the Internet predates the smartphone as I discovered reminiscing about my high school years and it's easy to become a zombie in front of any computer screen, whether desk-mounted or handheld, though the latter represents a deeper rabbit hole.

Setting and adhering to online limits hasn't always been easy. Many times I have found myself surfing the web on my laptop when I should have been doing work. Whether I was searching for an old classmate or checking out the weather forecast in Bora Bora, it was all a form of avoidance. Real work demands real concentration and I knew that. It also didn't take long for me to acknowledge that I was using the laptop as a replacement for the smartphone, so my habits needed even more refining.

Now I spend less than one hour of my leisure time each day on the Internet. As I don't own a television, I only spend about five leisure hours a week in front of all screens collectively. Other people I know have tried and failed to do the same, but they still have smartphones.

Taste of Freedom

My friend Lisa Esteban, a chaplain at a major hospital in New York City, has toyed with the idea of going back to a basic phone for years. Her job demands that she occasionally be on-call overnight, so she needs to decompress during her off hours. Her husband, Ed Esteban, works as a financial executive and at one point had not one but *two* mobile devices tied to work in addition to his personal smartphone. Like Lisa, he has considered downgrading (or upgrading, depending on your perspective) to a basic phone. What has held them back?

Lisa cited certain apps that make her feel safer, including one that screams in the event that the phone's owner is incapacitated. However, Lisa admitted that she has never needed to use the app and realizes that, faced with a violent confrontation, a person may not have the wherewithal to activate the feature. But Lisa has other less sinister reasons for choosing not to relinquish her phone. She and Ed are frequent travelers who cross the ocean at least once a year. There is no denying that smartphones make traveling easier, from eliminating the need to print a boarding pass to giving us real time updates on flight statuses. (During the Estebans' most recent vacation to Positano, Italy, however, they reported having spotty Internet access, so they might not have missed their iPhones very much.)

When I traveled out of state to visit a friend last month, I felt nervous about not having an iPhone anymore, which made me wonder – why can't we rent them? Short-term rentals abound in other markets. A designer ball gown or tuxedo can be yours for a night, you can clutch the keys to a Jaguar for the day, and you can hang out in a million dollar house in the Hamptons for a week – so why can't we do the same with smartphones? This hole in the rental market seems like a Kickstarter opportunity for a brave entrepreneur.

Lisa and I continued our friendly debate about technology as she confessed how a trip to Africa made her realize that she wanted to live without her phone, even though it doesn't seem realistic. Several years ago, she traveled with a group of Christian missionaries to rural Rwanda. During her three weeks in the impoverished country, Lisa walked miles a day to gather semi-clean water and returned in the evening to accommodations that had limited electricity and Internet. Lisa relayed how she dreaded returning to New York and had never felt more at peace than she did lying in her cot staring through the mosquito net into the darkness. No one she met had a mobile phone and, in an effort to fit in, she kept hers locked in a suitcase. She remarked about how "connected" people were and how conversations lasted hours rather than minutes. Lisa contrasted her time in Rwanda with a typical day in her life back home.

"It seems everyone's attention span has shortened dramatically and with that I believe their patience has as well. Conversations that used to be born while waiting for the elevators or walking through hallways have now been replaced by mindless scrolling that isolates us and also communicates a desire for distance. I think as a society, we are lonelier than we have ever been and I wonder how much we have participated in creating that loneliness with this device that distracts us and repels those who would be interested in engaging with us," she said.

Once again lost in the city shuffle, Lisa fell back to her routines of hourly smartphone monitoring and noted that she is "constantly policing" herself. As the Estebans hope to start a family, they have already laid down ground rules for how their children will access digital technology. The couple agrees that their children should not have access to any mobile device at least until the age of ten, at which point the kids would be equipped with basic phones for emergency purposes. I asked Lisa at what age her children would progress to smartphones and she replied without an ounce of humor, "When they can afford it."

Some may view her assertion as harsh while others will consider it a "Hallelujah" moment. Having worked part-time in high school to help purchase my first used car, I fall into the latter category. That '91 Plymouth Laser was the dictionary definition of a jalopy, but it was my hard-earned jalopy. I cared for the car with scheduled oil changes and tune-ups more than I would have done if it had been handed to me wrapped in red ribbons. Likewise, Lisa and Ed's children will almost certainly have more respect for their smartphones if obligated to work for them.

The Greatest

Honest work is one of the most salient lessons my father taught me and living without a smartphone helps me pay homage to him. Victor didn't live his life in breathless expectation of the next best thing. His life was lived as all our lives should be: with peace and contentment for what is and a steady diet of freedom rather than a mere taste. My father set an example and I daresay he would be proud to know that I have stepped off the digital bandwagon to live fully on my own terms.

Offline Solution #16: *Do you live according to your own rules? If not, what would it look like if you did? How could a taste of freedom become a gourmet meal? Let your imagination run wild...*

VELVET JOY

"Until one has loved an animal a part of one's soul remains
unawakened."
- Anatole France

*Buster Brown frolics through the warm Gulf waters, his tail
swishing above the waves as I wrap my arms around his mane and
rest my head against his strong neck. An apricot and amber dawn
streaks across a clear sky as the horse moves in closer to feel the heat
of the rising sun. The horse takes measured steps forward as I guide
him closer to the gritty sand where a bucket of water awaits. Buster
Brown drinks the cool water as I stare in awe at the fireball blazing
anew. All is silent except for the croons of gulls and the gentle horse
reaping his reward for serving as my earthly guardian angel
through the water.*

This sunrise horseback ride on the beach was how I rang
in January 1, 2019, and it kept me glued to the present

moment, unable to wax sentimental about the year behind or become nervous about the year ahead. Steering a horse through the Gulf of Mexico required all my focus. When we are in the company of animals, with their visceral reactions and earnest companionship, we have no other choice but to be present with them.

Though Buster Brown and your dog or cat don't know the words "mindfulness" or "meditation" they practice these concepts every moment of their lives. How is it that an animal can master the art of living in the present moment without even trying when ascetics spend years inching towards enlightenment? With only a subconscious understanding of the past – memories that might trigger fear or excitement – and no idea of the future beyond the instinct to survive, animals can teach us what it means to be grounded in the present moment.

Dolphin Calls

Animals show us how joyful and complete a life of simplicity can be – when their basic needs are met, they are more than content. But can we really emulate the quiet wisdom of animals? After all, we have far more responsibilities than they do (when was the last time your pampered pet paid the mortgage)? Our brains and therefore our needs are also more complicated.

Yes, we like to fancy ourselves standing proud at the top of the food chain, but we might feel differently if we stumbled into a tiger's lair. Similarly, we might consider our intelligence to be superior to that of all other beings, though there are countless ways to measure intellect, such as preservation of habitat, which places animals squarely ahead of the human race. The takeaway is that there are wildly diverse sentient beings on this mind-boggling planet and if we adopt a more flexible perspective, we can learn from them.

Susan Casey, dolphin aficionado and former editor of *O Magazine*, might agree. In her book, *Voices in the Ocean: A Journey into the Wild and Haunting World of Dolphins*, Casey writes:

> ...the mass of dolphins moved in fluid, constantly changing groups, much like people milling around at a cocktail party. This was a sophisticated arrangement, uncommon in nature, requiring the animals to recognize one another, form bonds, trade favors, recall past associations, and get along in unfamiliar circumstances.[1]

The elaborate behavior that Casey describes is attributable to the dolphins' unusually large and mysterious brains which scientists are only starting to decipher. What we do know is that dolphins have more neocortical neurons, associated with abilities like cognition and sensory perception, than any mammal including humans. What do dolphins do with all this intelligence?

For one, they live peaceful lives inasmuch as their environments and human intervention will allow. Dolphins only leave their harmonious salt water depths when an outside force, like a toxic oil spill, poses a threat. Then a dolphin may wash up on the shore, no longer rooted in the home environment that naturally facilitates peace. Are we like dolphins muscled ashore when technology infiltrates our lives the way chemicals poison theirs? If technology snatches away our peace of mind, then we are indeed like the dolphins.

Imbalances in the environment affect all animals, whether a house cat, grazing cow, or wild leopard. A driving factor behind this lack of equilibrium may be our fixation on the unnatural world. Stephanie Marohn, author of the book *What the Animals Taught Me*, proposes a solution, one that would certainly drag us away from our devices. She writes:

> Humans could not continue to destroy the natural world as we have so systematically been doing if we allowed ourselves to feel our innate connection with nature, instead of frantically amassing material goods, disappearing into addictions, and otherwise checking out to keep from feeling that connection.[2]

If you have ever dared to shop at the mall on Black Friday, then you know how materialistic our culture is. Marohn suggests that rather than "frantically amassing material goods," we should reconnect with nature, including animals. To accomplish that goal, it would be useful to remember that we never should have become disconnected from nature in the first place because *we are nature*. If we are disconnected from nature, then we are disconnected from ourselves. Conversely, when we shut down devices, we open up the window to nature, to ourselves, and to peace.

My favorite yoga studio displays a sign that declares the property to be a "cell phone free zone." If you do dare to bring your device into the studio, you will be subject to public humiliation through an irate teacher who will point you out and ask you to leave. I know this because it happened to me in my former days of digital obsession. Disgraced, I walked out of the studio and ran to my car where I stuffed the peace thief into the glove compartment. Though I was embarrassed, I knew the policy was wise. If we can't relax in a dark room with candles glowing and incense burning, then what hope is there? Fifteen years earlier, I had been drawn to the practice of yoga because of how relaxing it is, and there I was corrupting the atmosphere with a shrill handheld traffic light.

My teacher in another yoga class crystallized the notion of our phones serving as obstacles to peace. Danielle, a mother of two in her mid-thirties, described a solitary morning when she left the kids with their dad and drove to the beach to practice yoga. She chose Siesta Key Beach in Sarasota, Florida, not an obvious choice for someone seeking tranquility. This beach has been ranked number one in the nation in more surveys than a mathematician could count. Tourists from as far away as Eastern Europe flock there like pilgrims to dip their toes in the fine quartz sand of the wide shoreline. Thumping drum circles, kids with chocolate swirl ice cream dribbling down their chins, and wall-to-wall sunbathers lend a party atmosphere to Siesta Key. Danielle, however, found a slice of paradise that morning, thanks to a little bird.

The slender white egret danced on the sand within reach of where Danielle sat and stretched. As the bird lingered, she paused her practice and started to observe. She recounted to the class, "It's as if the egret was telling me to watch and listen and not do anything else. It was definitely a photo-op moment at that close range and I would have been trying to get a shot if I had my phone with me. Luckily I didn't, so I just stayed there in silent awe, as almost forty-five minutes passed on my watch and the egret was still doing its little dance."

Offline Solution #17: *The next time you're outside, observe a bird, squirrel, or other wildlife in its natural environment. Note three specific things you noticed that could be metaphorical for how you live. For example, is the animal in a hurry? If not, then maybe the message is to slow down. Try to resist the temptation to* *photograph the animal. Instead, sketch a picture of the scene in your mind to recall when you need an infusion of peace.*

Peaceful Pets

AND WHAT ABOUT OUR PETS? What can they teach us about the peace that the present moment carries? Our pets comprehend enough to process and follow commands, express love, and even warn us of impending danger. (Have you ever been stuck in a house with two Chihuahuas when a stranger rings the doorbell late at night? Lucky you.) So, we ought to trust our pets enough to show us how to experience a better quality of life through leisure and engagement.

Even knowing that our brains are more intricate than those of our feline and canine buddies, can we still absorb a lesson or two from their mindful behavior? Consider cat naps. Cats spend an inordinate portion of their lives (up to two-thirds) asleep as some seek after a REM cycle eighteen hours a day. While we're not going to cat nap our way through life, we can pause for an hour each day and turn everything off – our devices and our minds simultaneously.

Like a feathery white Turkish Angora, we can laze in the sun, curl up on the couch, or sprawl out on the bed without any guilt. We may need to fight the compulsion to do other things, and to check one very irksome thing in particular, but we can repossess our downtime as what it is – sacred. In fact, in an age when many employers are demanding 24/7 access to employees, our downtime has never been more precious. It may be easier said than done, but as a society of workers we can shift employers' expectations of this soul-sucking nonstop availability. How? By reclaiming our free time without apology or explanation. Oh, and by turning off those Slack notifications.

And then there's playtime. If you have ever played fetch with a sprinting dog, you know how gripping the game is for Mr. Flufferson. There is nothing more enrapturing than that Frisbee flying across the lawn. The dog is both focused on and delighted with exactly what he is doing, precisely in that irreplaceable moment in time. Therein lies a key lesson: we can retrieve the Frisbee for our pet, but we can never retrieve the moment.

I have a most unusual cat named Rainbow who plays "tennis" with her stuffed toy mice. I toss a mouse to her and she bats it back to me with her paw. She could play this game for hours if I had the patience. Now I am more focused when I play with my pet, but before I would check my iPhone periodically, interrupting the nonverbal communication that can blossom between humans and domesticated animals. If a cat could be envious, then Rainbow was, scrunching up her tiny face and strutting out of the room whenever I would reach for the iPhone.

As adults we rarely engage in such carefree play. When was the last time you were immersed in play – perhaps as a curious child? It's no secret that as adults we have lost our play skills – or have we merely exchanged them? Are video games, online trivia, gambling, and interactive social match-ups more intriguing to us than our real world hobbies?

A Baby Boomer acquaintance who shall remain nameless used to play golf in his spare time. He was a smart saver throughout his career as an electrician and never so much as glimpsed the inside of a casino. Since a smartphone slammed into his lane, he has chucked the golf clubs in exchange for online gambling. This middle class man, recently retired, has squandered a tragic amount of his nest egg banking on virtual slot machines that have brought him pairs of lemons rather than those elusive triple sevens. At seventy-two years old, he has very little chance of earning (or winning) back that lost money. Golf is not a cheap hobby, but it is a healthy one that keeps players on their feet whereas online gambling steals cash and well-being alike.

I haven't lost any cash on digital gaming, but I have certainly sacrificed my well-being. When I was under the influence of the smartphone, I neglected my playful pastimes like salsa dancing and stand-up paddle boarding. Instead I zoned out for hours playing quiz games with strangers from around the world, a sad virtual replica of my childhood days gathered around a Trivial Pursuit board with friends in the flesh. I was involved in the online quiz games and yet not present like Buster Brown wading through the water or your dog catching a squeaky ball in her mouth. My mind, not to mention my vision, was cloudy as I went through the motions of the game like it was an out-of-body experience, the total opposite of the raw pleasure my chocolate horse felt at first light.

Being physically in a place does not mean we are present. Even being mentally in a place does not equate with true presence. Presence is experienced on a higher and deeper level, as an offering of our spirits, of our whole selves to whomever or whatever engages us in that very moment, as though nothing existed before and nothing will follow after. Pet a purring cat and you'll get a clear, tangible idea of what presence means. Trap your phone under lock and key for two hours and you'll arrive at the same understanding.

Lessons from a Blind Cat

Once a week I volunteer at a shelter that houses more than three dozen abandoned cats. My official job title is Pet Socializer as I am charged with earning each animal's trust through gentle but steady interaction, thus preparing them for successful adoption. I invariably become attached to the cats and vice versa, and I'm always amazed at how solicitous they are of my company. There are no dinging, beeping, burping devices to tear their attention away. There is no text that urges an instant reply, no missed calls, no spam emails. There is just the moment shared between a loving human and an astute animal, a bundle of velvet joy who is at liberty to savor every moment the way moments were designed to be savored.

String Bean has been one of my greatest teachers at the shelter. Blind since birth, this black and white cat (whose wimpy name is a misnomer as he is the feline equivalent of Hercules) vocalizes his needs and relies on his nose to do all the rest. Special needs pets tend to be adopted last and String Bean was no exception. After months of stealing volunteers' hearts, String Bean received a visit from a family with two young children. The parents were skeptical about adopting a blind cat and the children were also wary as the little boy commented, "How will he watch YouTube with me on my iPad?" I smiled and replied that adopting a cat like String Bean meant that there would be a lot less time to spend watching videos. The cat's needs would have to come first and String Bean would be a big responsibility, I explained.

The parents' ears perked up as soon as they heard me say, "less time to spend watching videos." A short discussion between the mother and father led to their decision to adopt String Bean that day. I knew that integrating this special pet into the family would mean that the iPad would take a back seat and the parents knew it too. Both children would benefit from sharing the caretaking duties of a vulnerable animal. Was I too optimistic to suppose that they might completely lose interest in their devices? Perhaps. But regardless, one cat's "handicap" turned out to be a priceless gift for two impressionable children.

Friendship with an animal schools us in compassion and softens us into baby-talking piles of marshmallow fluff. Animals help us attain the true connection that we are seeking in this chilly "modern world" that Bradley Cooper and Lady Gaga sing about in "Shallow" from the blockbuster film *A Star Is Born*. The lyrics ring true as we are all searching for something more than the digital realm provides. That something more just may be found in the trusting eyes of an animal.

9

EMERALD GREEN

"Nature does not hurry, yet everything is accomplished."
- Lao Tzu

JULY 2017. Summer rain had been falling for days. I strolled through the park where trees reflected like emeralds against the clearing sky. A sandhill crane hopped into my path as an enigmatic bird glided overhead. Buzzing, not from a bird or bumblebee, shattered the peace. Glaring, I pulled my phone out of my pocket and the idyllic wonders vanished into the ether...

Have you ever been enjoying some much needed time with Mother Nature when Father Technology barges onto the scene? As a woman, I was conditioned to keep my cell phone with me at all times "just in case" of an emergency. You may have other reasons for hauling your phone with you into the great outdoors. But consider leaving your phone in the glove compartment the next time you go for a walk. If you're going for a solo hike or entering into isolated terrain, then by all means bring the phone. But if you're just roaming around town in daylight hours, give yourself permission to savor every moment. Who knows? You might become a forest lord.

Sebastian is only four years old, but he is already a forest lord of the highest order. For the past year, Sebastian has studied among the Pacific silver firs and western hemlocks that grow taller than skyscrapers in Washington State. He lives in Maple Valley, a suburb of Seattle and the home of Lake Wilderness Forest School. The forty-acre grounds surrounding crystalline Lake Wilderness comprise Sebastian's classroom. Sebastian's school days involve hands-on play, discovery, and buckets of fresh air. The fun doesn't end in the summer as Sebastian is enrolled in a nature camp at the forest school where he digs for "dinosaur bones" and fossils.

I visited Lake Wilderness Forest School in May of 2018 when I was in Maple Valley housesitting for Sebastian's parents, who are longtime friends of mine. Before my friends departed on a family vacation to Paris, I had the good fortune of discovering the school on a most unusual graduation day. The ceremony took place in the heart of the forest in the midst of a bone-chilling drizzle. Following a potluck brunch set up on picnic tables and blankets, the children prepared to receive their accolades. Oblivious to the rain and mud, the excited graduates lined up and one by one climbed to the top of a very small hill. When each child reached the top, the teachers would ask: "Are you ready to jump into summer?" Sebastian and his giggling classmates answered with a resounding "Yes!" as they took the symbolic leap from the hill to the grass.

At the start of the ceremony, the forest school teachers had requested that parents refrain from photography. "We'll be taking pictures of your child and you'll have a keepsake photograph with their diplomas!" A teacher assured cheerfully, her unkempt honey hair tossing in the wind.

You can imagine what happened next. Of course no one listened. Of course the proud parents took photos from every angle, not missing a moment of the ceremony, yet missing them all. The children hardly noticed the phones flashing in their faces. Perhaps it's because they were so joyful with the crisp Pacific Northwest air at their backs, or maybe they were so accustomed to the devices that they didn't notice them anymore.

Either way, the children were in their element and the teachers were gifting them a more valuable education than the ones that happen inside four walls. Next year when Sebastian turns five, he will be home-schooled and his younger brother, Luke, will take his place at the forest school. Neither Sebastian nor Luke has access to any mobile device and their mother monitors how much television they watch. Together, the boys gather for a family movie on most afternoons in the living room. Following the film, they return to their massive book collection and an art room filled with chalks, paints, and crayons. The boys are enriched but not overstimulated; moreover, Sebastian exhibits an exceptional attention span for a child who is barely beyond the toddler stage. He looked me deep in the eyes during every conversation we had, listening to my perspective and making appropriate contributions of his own. The topics may have been juvenile, like how he couldn't wait to pull Luke in a wagon down the block, but the level of communication was sophisticated.

His imagination is equally impressive. Fluff from cottonwood trees is freshly fallen snow; the reclusive housecat is a jungle superhero. Sebastian is a master storyteller in the making and an abstract painter in training. He benefits from the presence of two caring parents who don't use their devices to excess. Add in the fact that Sebastian has not yet been introduced to a smartphone and the recipe for success is obvious.

Sebastian's childhood stands in contrast to many children who begin using screens during their toddler years or even younger. Brad Huddleston, who has a degree in computer science, authored the book *Digital Cocaine: A Journey Toward iBalance*. In an interview with *Vero's Voice* magazine, Huddleston points out:

> ...Medication with Ritalin and other similar drugs are just flowing like M&Ms around the world. ADHD is up 800 percent...that screen is causing hyperstimulation in the brain. Essentially, it's an artificial environment and the brain cannot cope...[1]

The wilderness environment of Sebastian's forest school could not be more of a departure from the artificial environment Huddleston evokes. Sebastian and his forest school classmates are engaged in tangible, get-your-hands-dirty tasks from the second they step into the woods. In a way, Sebastian is the proverbial *Last Child in the Woods* depicted by Richard Louv in his 2005 book. *Last Child in the Woods* introduces the concept of nature deficit disorder as Louv argues that 21st century youngsters need more recreational time outdoors. While nature deficit disorder may not be a formal medical diagnosis, it is certainly valid when we consider how little time the majority of children spend outdoors compared to prior generations. The National Recreation and Park Association puts this fact into disheartening perspective, noting that the current generation of youth devotes an average of only four to seven *minutes* to outdoor play per day! On the other hand, the organization reports that these same children spend more than seven *hours* on electronic media per day.[2] Establishing a link between these statistics and childhood obesity, the National Recreation and Park Association has urged Congress to act with legislation that supports reconnecting youth with nature.

The fact that we need a law to ensure that children get adequate fresh air and exercise is testament to how detrimental screens are to human growth and development. Thankfully, the remedy is free and available to everyone. Just step outside and take your medicine.

From Forest School to Forest Bathing

You may be too old for forest school, but you are never too old for forest bathing. Called *shinrin-yoku* in Japanese, the practice of forest bathing is ancient, but the contemporary concept developed in Japan in the 1980s when companies like Sony and Hitachi were in their prime. Overwhelmed Japanese businesspeople, and anyone who lived near frenetic Tokyo, needed a break from the demands of society. What better way to counteract the relentless drone of electronics and the pressures of the modern work day than by drawing a bath in the forest? There's no soap or loofah or body wash required for this kind of bath. All you need are your five senses and a desire to separate from technology while rejoining nature.

Dr. Qing Li eats his lunch every day in a park near the medical school where he works in Tokyo. This physician and chairman of the Japanese Society for Forest Medicine also spends a more concentrated three days each month practicing *shinrin-yoku* in the woods of Japan, claiming that these forest baths wield power against diseases of civilization including gastric ulcers and anxiety.[3] Across the map in Europe, the Duchess of Cambridge (informally known as Kate Middleton, wife of Prince William) practices her own style of forest bathing. The Duchess has an affinity for gardening and has reportedly entered her arrangements in the famed Chelsea Flower Show.[4]

Whether it's an English garden or a Japanese forest, these restorative baths are easy, free ways to reclaim our peace. In his book, *Forest Bathing: How Trees Can Help You Find Health and Happiness*, Li writes:

> By opening our senses, it bridges the gap between us and the natural world. And when we are in harmony with the natural world we can begin to heal. Our nervous system can reset itself, our bodies and minds can go back to how they ought to be.[5]

And what if we don't live near a forest? Li does admit that most Japanese live in urban or suburban environments just as an overwhelming majority (80 percent) of Americans do. So, a daily two-hour hike through a forest might be ideal, but it's far from feasible. However, some of our cities have preserved an encouraging amount of green space. New York City boasts eight hundred forty acres of Central Park; Chicago has its eighteen-mile Lakefront Trail; and Cincinnati maintains the hilltop refuge of Eden Park. You might not see too many woodland critters at an urban park and you might not smell a wave of minty pine, but you can still reap some of the same rewards as forest bathers do.

Offline Solution #18: *Visit a park in your community. Walk to the park if possible and bring a brown bag lunch or picnic basket feast. Notice the difference in the air quality as you breathe in abundant oxygen from the trees. Explore other parks in your area until you find a favorite. Then, try to reserve an hour or two each* *week to visit the park and walk among the trees for a modified version of forest bathing.*

EVEN LOOKING at photographs of nature can have a calming effect, Li claims. If you own a coffee table book of beach, wildlife, or aerial photographs, then you probably already know this. A view of trees from a bedroom or office window can energize the senses as well. Hospital patients recover more rapidly when their room faces a green area. One study showed that patients who either gazed at a tree from their hospital room windows or perused photographs of nature needed less pain medication than other patients.[6]

These facts may not come across as astounding, but what is more jarring is Li's comparison of natural versus artificial sounds and their implications for our moods. Citing a study from England's Brighton and Sussex Medical School, Li explains the outcomes for the participants:

> The results showed that when participants listened to artificial sounds, their attention was focused inwards. Inward-focused attention is associated with worry and brooding. When they listened to the sounds of nature, they turned their attention outwards.[7]

The researchers' observations delineate the opposite poles of narcissism and altruism. On one hand manmade noise, like the chirp of an incoming text message, not only makes people focus on themselves but thrusts the focus into a negative light. On the other hand natural sounds, like birdsong and falling rain, propel us beyond ourselves and uplift us into a state of relaxed equilibrium, as Li goes on to describe. We recoil into ourselves with our devices and we become depressed. We retreat into nature and the whole world opens up to us, and vice versa.

Since 1999 and the Columbine tragedy, sociologists and medical professionals have debated whether or not violent video games precede violent actions. We as a society have passionately engaged in the same dispute. Ask Google "do video games cause violence?" and the search engine will retrieve more than 73 million contradictory results. Some studies fail to demonstrate a link between gaming and aggression, while other research asserts that there could be a connection. If we are to draw a parallel between the Brighton study and the inner world of video gamers, we could argue that since they are at greater risk of "worry and brooding," then they might be more likely to act out. This book does not seek to answer a question that has thus far been unanswerable, but I would like to pose a new question: does bonding with nature and shunning artificial sounds, light, and scenarios make us *less* violent?

The Environmental Dilemma

A different sort of aggression towards the environment takes place in the factories where smartphones are assembled for mass distribution. In short, there's nothing green about how your iPhone was manufactured. The problems start in the earliest stages of production. It's not emeralds that comprise a smartphone but other types of rare and precious metals, such as gold. Industrial gold mining is a dirty practice that produces tons of toxic waste which seep into the environment. To be fair, computers may contain gold as well, but we don't generally buy a new computer every year. Further, while 262 million personal computers were purchased in 2017, a staggering 1.5 billion smartphones were purchased that same year, one for every five people alive on the planet.[8] What will those billions of people do with their billions of phones after the next tantalizing product release?

(As I write this chapter, the iPhone 11 is about to smack the shelves like a tidal wave.)

Gold is not the only metal mined to make our devices. Iron, aluminum and copper mining create their own set of woes for the environment and, consequently, for human health. In 2015, a dam collapse in Brazil killed nineteen people and released a deluge of toxic waste from iron mining into the Atlantic Ocean.[9] Why do swordfish and sharks have such high levels of mercury in their bodies? Water pollution is the obvious answer, but where does it come from? Mercury is one more element used to produce smartphones and is found in the device's battery, crystal display, and circuit board.[10] If these materials are harmful for wildlife, waterways, and land, then they are harmful for us too. Compound the environmental cost with the planned obsolescence that makes us "need" a new phone every year or two and you've got a toxic wasteland.

Senior technology writer Mark Wilson discusses this issue in an eye-opening article for *Fast Company* magazine. In his article, "Smartphones Are Killing the Planet Faster Than Anyone Expected," he writes:

> Smartphones are particularly insidious for a few reasons. With a two-year average life cycle, they're more or less disposable. The problem is that building a new smartphone – and specifically, mining the rare materials inside them – represents 85 percent to 95 percent of the device's CO2 emissions for two years. That means buying one new phone takes as much energy as recharging and operating a smartphone for an entire decade.[11]

Indeed, the disposable culture to which Wilson alludes is part of the problem. We "delete" people from our contacts and social media profiles with one tap and we do the same with our belongings. Holding onto any of our possessions longer, from furniture to dinnerware, promotes a greener earth. One could argue that smartphones are compact and have replaced the need for other bulkier items like alarm clocks, cameras and stereo systems. But how often did you actually replace those things? Alarm clocks aren't much fun to shop for and unless you're a professional photographer you probably didn't buy a new camera every eighteen months. My father, who had a love affair with classical music, kept the same stereo system for almost thirty years. There's a reason that his was hailed as the Greatest Generation. Maybe those Baby Boomer, Generation X, and Millennial technology executives should enroll in forest school next fall.

Offline Solution #19: *Less than 1 percent of smartphones are recycled.[12] Be a green warrior and bring your old cell phone to a recycling or donation center in your neighborhood. Or partner with a company like Best Buy, Staples, or Office Depot which offer buyback options and/or savings incentives. Recycle the lithium-ion battery of your phone separately; to find a drop-off location near you, visit call2recycle.org and enter your zip code. Did you know that you can also recycle your old television, tablet, and laptop? Almost everything we use can be used again if we recycle.*

The Jewel of Childhood

THE RETIREMENT COMMUNITY in South Jersey seemed on the surface an unlikely place to start a nature club. The houses were a bit too tidy and cookie cutter and a pretentious golf course cut through the open land. But as an overeager child with an overactive imagination, I thought the idea was ingenious (though my name for the group, the Nature Club, was absolutely yawn-worthy). In 1989, I founded the Nature Club with a five dollar donation from my Uncle Steve and the blessing of my mother. As a club/family, we took walks around the trail surrounding the golf course; donned our orange life jackets to row through the lake; and picked up shells and washed up starfish that we discovered in our beachcombing at the infamous Jersey Shore. To this day, the Nature Club is an inside joke in my family and I assure my uncle each year that his original five dollar donation has earned him the status of lifetime member.

The Nature Club fed and expanded my love of the outdoors. Shortly after I established the club, my parents signed up for an eight-mile walkathon called "Walk for Watershed" to save the empty land surrounding a local reservoir from construction cranes and real estate moguls. My mother, a Baby Boomer channeling her inner flower child, held up a sign that said "don't pave paradise" in hot pink letters while I slurped orange slices from the rest stations along the way.

Mom and Dad nourished my love of the outdoors even when I protested. Raking leaves and shoveling snow were seasonal chores that I couldn't escape, but the reward was a cup of Swiss Miss hot chocolate stuffed to the brim with mini marshmallows. I preferred walking to hiking, because the latter was too strenuous, but my father encouraged me to take up the exhilarating sport. From a fallen branch in our backyard, he fashioned a hiking stick and fitted a rubber cap on the top so splinters wouldn't get into my hands. Once I had my hiking stick, I was ready to be a mountaineer.

These memories are the jewel in the crown of my childhood. Today I am as enamored of nature as I was when I brainstormed the Nature Club's first outing. My uncle, the founding club member, now resides in the Berkshire

Mountains of Massachusetts on two rural acres of property complete with a pebbly creek and herb garden. If you have ever been to the Berkshires, you know that every square foot of land is like a cover photo from *Field & Stream*. Visiting him and his wife, Charlotte, at their rustic house sends me back to my emerald green youth and the best memories, most of which were spent outdoors. I imagine that Sebastian the forest lord will one day remember his childhood with similar fondness.

ARTIST'S COBBLESTONE PATH

"Every human is an artist. And this is the main art that we
have: the creation of our story."
- Don Miguel Ruiz

IN 1955, a weary wife and mother of five decided that she
needed some time alone. She packed a few belongings and
disappeared to southwest Florida's Captiva Island, a chain of
pristine beaches notable for its variety of seashells. Each day
she refilled her own well, living simply in a waterfront
cottage with bare walls and the plainest furniture. The
cottage's only adornments were driftwood and leaves that the
author gathered on the shore. She walked to the beach every
day, sometimes with a picnic lunch and other times with just
a pen and notebook.

This vacation provided the basis for Anne Morrow
Lindbergh's contemplative book *Gift from the Sea* in which she
depicts the necessity of undistracted solitude. She also

laments how women of her generation escaped into television soap operas and other frivolities instead of cherishing their time alone. The author writes:

> Even daydreaming was more creative than this; it demanded something of oneself and it fed the inner life. Now, instead of planting our solitude with our own dream blossoms, we choke the space with continuous music, chatter and companionship to which we do not even listen. It is simply there to fill the vacuum.[1]

Do her seaside musings resonate with you? In the 1950s, people were distracting themselves with the "boob tube" or "idiot box" as television sets came into vogue. Radio programs were another diversion. Today we have a confounding array of media to choose from, making television and radio seem almost quaint in the midst of interminable social networking and gaming channels. The methods of distraction have changed, but the principle has remained the same. It is easier to step outside ourselves, ignoring what is transpiring in our hearts and minds in favor of watching other people live their train wreck lives. How else could reality shows have become so absurdly popular? Rather than pointing and laughing at such uncouth scripted puppet shows, we might seek that restorative solitude of which Morrow Lindbergh wrote.

I can only imagine how Anne Morrow Lindbergh's sabbatical would have worked if it took place in 2015 rather than 1955. Certainly, she would have left her iPhone at home in Connecticut. And if she hadn't, then she may not have succeeded in writing her classic book that has inspired millions of women globally with its translation into forty-five languages. Not only would she have been hopelessly distracted, but the thoughts may indeed not have trickled into her mind and onto paper at all. By disengaging herself from the outside world, she reconnected with nature and adopted a flowing daily rhythm that spilled over into her writing. Morrow Lindbergh's daughter, Reeve, wrote the introduction to the fiftieth anniversary edition of *Gift from the Sea* and characterizes her mother's writing as "...the easy, inevitable movements of the sea."[2]

Most of us do not have the luxury of abandoning our responsibilities for a week, let alone several, to gallivant off to a private island. We can, however, reserve time each day to indulge in a mini retreat. Bypass the cafeteria at lunch and take a walk outside. Go to the gym for an hour on Saturday morning. Or, better yet, do nothing at all and open yourself to the creativity that might come gushing through the flood gates. But it is not easy to attain the bliss of nothingness when we're crowded out with noise and clutter.

Offline Solution #20: *Pare down your belongings and do a closet clean-out. You may have several storage areas that need tidying, but focus on one for today. Establish rules for what you will keep, donate or sell. For example, if you haven't worn that shirt in more than a year, maybe it's time to let it go. If you want to do an extreme closet makeover, you can try to reduce your possessions to a round number of one hundred. Dave Bruno shares how he made friends with minimalism in his book, The 100-Thing Challenge: How I Got Rid of Almost Everything, Remade My Life, and Regained My Soul. As an alternative, turn this activity into a mental exercise and discern which hundred belongings you would keep if faced with the choice.*

Voluntary Exile

NEARLY A DECADE after Anne Morrow Lindbergh had her sunny sojourn in Florida, another Anne sought refuge in the wilds. In 1964, New Jersey native Anne LaBastille built a log cabin in a section of the Adirondack Mountains so remote that it could only be accessed by boat. Her cabin was not equipped with electricity, plumbing or a telephone. She wrote her books on a legal pad, used an outhouse, and walked over a mile to get her mail. Her life was simple and for many, undesirable and downright dangerous.

Armed with a German shepherd and a shotgun, thirty-something LaBastille was conscious of her vulnerability in that lone cabin. She was resourceful, living in harmony with the raw materials of the land rather than exploiting them. She was also very prolific. LaBastille went on to earn a Ph.D. in wildlife ecology from Cornell University and to write a successful series of four memoirs titled *Woodswoman*. In between international travel for various conservation projects, including one to save the now extinct giant grebe birds of Guatemala, LaBastille authored books until 2003 when she turned seventy years old.

LaBastille died in 2011 when a minority of the population had adopted smartphones and it is safe to say that she never touched one. Nor would she have wanted to if we are to draw inferences from her own words:

> ...visions of uninterrupted mornings sitting at my desk, quiet evenings rocking by the stove, and living a simple and totally private life lured me unerringly to my new home. The first evening I ate supper on the dock bathed by a golden sunset. A Rusty Blackbird creaked out his call from an alder bush and two Purple Finches warbled atop a tall spruce. Not a breath of wind ruffled the water.[3]

LaBastille drew inspiration from her natural surroundings, not from a television program. Her evocative language illustrates her sheer contentment to live unchained from technology and society while her story brings to mind another more famous cabin dweller, Henry David Thoreau. The association might not be a stretch as Justin Housman recognized when he penned the article, "Anne LaBastille May Have Out-Thoreau'd Thoreau" for *Adventure Journal*. Housman paints a vibrant picture of LaBastille and her not-so-secret admirers:

> Many men who'd read her work became enthralled with a blonde Daisy Duke-wearing, tough-as-nails mountain woman living a rustic writer's life in a cabin, and would seek her out at the lake, bearing gifts, occasionally marriage proposals.[4]

More than a century before LaBastille's escapades as a woodswoman, Thoreau wrote the nature memoir, *Walden*, which is perhaps the quintessential literary lesson in the value of simplicity. In this introspective volume, Thoreau recounts the two years in which he constructed a cabin, grew beans, and lived a blissfully basic life off the land. Could Thoreau have written *Walden* if he had been the target of a perpetually vibrating contraption on his painted pine desk? Even this transcendentalist master probably wouldn't have been immune to such distractions. In fact, Thoreau isolated himself in a cabin at Walden Pond in Massachusetts precisely so he could focus on his writing project.

On a smaller scale, I was doing the same when I decided that my life would be more fruitful without a smartphone. Obviously, this book would not have been written had I not given up my smartphone because the subject matter wouldn't exist, but I doubt that I would have written *any* book if I had kept the device in my possession. Prior to this project, I had been churning out snappy eight hundred-word articles and five hundred-word blog posts for clients. These micro-projects required just enough time and attention that I could write them in an hour or two – and then go back to worshipping my phone.

Juxtapose that short attention span with my youth when I spent uninterrupted hours writing with blue ink in spiral notebooks. I filled at least one thick diary every year with my youthful impressions. I molded blocks of colored clay into abstract sculptures that no one could identify. My mother taught me how to sew a stuffed fabric doll from a pattern that we drew ourselves. I learned how to read music and play the violin, screeching my way through more than a few school concerts.

I didn't have a particular talent for art or music, but that wasn't the point. My days were filled with endless creativity, the kind that satisfies the soul. My old-fashioned parents probably wouldn't have allowed me to have a smartphone if such technology had existed during my childhood. If by chance I had gotten my hands on one, I would surely have fallen prey to its clutches exactly the way the children of today have. I wouldn't have rehearsed for hours on the violin or nurtured the vegetable garden that grew in our side yard. I probably wouldn't be grateful for simple delights either, such as feeling the first spring rains or nibbling salt water taffy on the boardwalk.

Like my affinity for art, gratitude and love of simplicity were instilled in me from the beginning. One of the best presents I ever received as a kid was a metal weaving loom with a bag of rainbow colored loops. I would happily pass an afternoon threading the loops in each row to create heirloom potholders that I gave to the women in my family. Again, this is not to give the impression that I was crafty or innately gifted in art. I wasn't at all. My potholders were riddled with messy knots and hideous color combinations like pumpkin orange and pea green. But the artistic bug bit me anyway and complemented my school learning, occupying my free hours in a healthy and constructive way.

Offline Solution #21: *Take a few moments to reminisce about your childhood. What types of creative things did you do? What types of creative things do you do now? If you haven't been creative since your youth, what's holding you back? Break through the barriers and pick a fun project to work on; choose a simple one to delight your inner child. Doodle, color, sketch, finger paint to your heart's content.*

Portrait of a Contemporary Artist – Sans Smartphone

COLE MACDOUGLAS IS a mixed media artist who gathers natural and discarded materials to create his three-dimensional works. Born in Glasgow, Scotland, he has an Instagram account for his eclectic art yet he has never used the app himself. MacDouglas, who is in his sixties, chooses to use a flip phone without data access and claims that it helps him stay focused on his art.

When I sat down with MacDouglas on a humid summer day in his south Florida studio, he shared his insights about the creative process. My opening question earned a laugh from the artist.

"How many times a day do you check your phone?"

"Never! There's no need to check it. If it rings, then I know I have an incoming call because nobody texts me.

Otherwise the phone stays in the back room." He pointed to a closed door behind a paint-splattered easel.

"Have you ever thought about getting a smartphone?" I asked.

More laughter. "No, because I feel it would take away from my creativity. It would be a distraction. It's easy enough to get distracted from a challenging project without one of those phones as an added nuisance."

I glanced around at MacDouglas's studio and counted no fewer than four dozen individual pieces of art. There were driftwood carvings adorned with silk flowers, abstract sculptures of human figures, and vivid acrylic paintings in all sizes. Clearly, he was doing something right.

"How do you feel about technology in general and how it's changed the art world?" I inquired.

MacDouglas appeared pensive as he replied, "I think in many ways it's enhanced the art world because it's given artists a free forum that they wouldn't otherwise have had. It allows us to sell our work online and court potential buyers from all over the world. On the other hand, I don't like what it's done to photography. I'm not going to use one of those...what do you call them? The things people use to change photos?"

"Filters," I provided.

"Yes, one of those filters to doctor up my art and make it appear as something it isn't. Manipulating photographs of art for sale is false advertising and it compromises the integrity of the art form."

MacDouglas's observation made me think about how people manipulate photographs of themselves in much the same way, especially on dating websites. A flawless photograph of the self that resembles nothing of reality also equates to false advertising. Then, I reflected on the eco-writer and nature photographer, Tim Palmer, who refuses to edit his pictures. As Palmer writes in the personal statement on his website:

> I do not use Photoshop or any other means of manipulating my pictures after I take them. I do not change the color or content of my images in any way. I like to show what is actually there. I don't like the idea of people looking at pretty photos with amped-up colors and then heading out into the real natural world and being disappointed by what they see.[5]

Reality more than suffices for Palmer's awe-inspiring collection of photographs featuring the trees and rivers of North America. There is nothing disappointing about gazing at a full-color photograph of a 1,200-year-old Sierra Redwood in its raw splendor. On the wall of MacDouglas's studio, a painting of a windswept beach caught my eye and I thought how the two artists might be kindred spirits.

MacDouglas's final thought during the interview stripped away the need to ask if he would get a smartphone in the future. "I've never had a strong interest in technology and feel that my art is more organic and truthful without it."

As I stepped out into the stifling summer heat, I wondered how contemporary art and photography would be different if everyone were so honest.

Cheating on a Challenge?

And what about that gutsy gal who relinquished her smartphone for the promise of a six-figure payday from Vitaminwater? Elana A. Mugdan is a thirty-year-old film director and fantasy fiction writer from New York City. Besides the obvious lure of cash, Mugdan has said that she took on the challenge to focus on her writing and finish a series of self-published books.

Mugdan also revealed in an interview with CNBC that, "I really need to get better with the human interaction aspect of my life. I think being without the phone and having to navigate the social waters on my own without the use of technology will be a really great learning experience for me, actually."[6]

Oddly enough, Mugdan was still active on social media when I sat down to write this chapter in July of 2019. Since being selected to complete the challenge in February 2019, she has posted almost daily on her Twitter and Instagram accounts. One curious Instagram user addressed this issue with Mugdan in a post comment on July 18, 2019:

> **zen_curves:** Hey, I read that you were giving up your smartphone for a year. Not sure how that is possible with all your activity on Instagram?[7]

Elana Mugdan, with her Instagram user name officialdragonspeaker, "liked" the comment and replied less than an hour later according to the time stamp:

> **officialdragonspeaker:** @zen_curves you are correct! The smartphone is gone for good, but there are plenty of Instagram Chrome extensions that allow you to post via desktop computer, which has allowed me to keep up here – however, it's also true that I've drastically reduced the time I spend on the website! I post and I get out xD[8]

Social media ignoramus that I am, I had to look up that "xD" abbreviation at the end of Mugdan's response. According to various Internet slang dictionaries, the "x" represents eyes and the "D" symbolizes a smile. When

combined, the two letters are the equivalent of a laughing face
– or something to that effect. Writing "ha ha ha!" would be so
much easier for everyone, don't you think? In any case,
Mugdan's continued use of social media seemed a bit like
cheating, especially since the challenger shared with a
national media source how she sought to become more
sociable without the crutch of technology. Her yearlong
journey would seem more authentic perhaps if she resided in
a Thoreau-esque cabin without access to online loopholes
like Google Chrome extensions. Rather than a cobblestone
path, it seems like this city woman is traveling on a freshly
paved road free of potholes. On another token, Mugdan's
resourcefulness demonstrates that even social media fanatics
don't need a smartphone to stay connected.

> **Offline Solution #22:** *No one is paying you or me one penny to
> give up our phones or to use them less, but we can make it worth
> the effort by diving into a creative project. For beginner artists,
> Cole MacDouglas suggests experimenting with a set of oil paints in
> pastel shades. In lieu of a canvas, a piece of blank paper would
> work and MacDouglas recommends "letting the movement flow as
> you feel the colors and the emotions of the colors." Pale blue, for
> example, is a moody color, while light yellow evokes happiness and
> dusty rose hints at romance. An alternative project without the
> need to purchase supplies would be to scavenge at a nearby beach,
> lake, river, or brook. Gather pebbles, driftwood, shells, anything
> you find and create a collage of natural objects.*

THE ARTIST'S path is a solitary one paved in cobblestones. We
don't need any artistic talent to travel this path. We don't need
to enroll in an art class. We don't even need any particular

tools or supplies. All we need are our imaginations, a little time to ourselves, and a whole lot of honesty. We may never paint like Monet or sculpt like Rodin, but we will hear the voice of the muse when we tune out the cacophony that wants to overtake us.

MIND & BODY IN SYNCH

"Nothing is as important as reconnecting with your bliss.
Nothing is as rich. Nothing is as real."
- Deepak Chopra

DUST off that old photo album and board your invisible time machine to the innocence of childhood. Do you remember how you used to answer that ubiquitous question: what do you want to be when you grow up? Most likely, your childhood imagination spun a multitude of answers that shifted during the growing seasons of your youth. My mother recorded a memory book of kindergarten through twelfth grade with each page surveying vital statistics such as height and weight as well as documenting what I wanted to be when I grew up. We recently unearthed this book from her storage closet and I was surprised by the variety of career interests I had as a kid:

Kindergarten: Gymnast in the Olympics
First Grade: Doctor
Second Grade: Traveling Photographer
Third Grade: Florist
Fourth Grade: Work in an office (the first and last time I ever had that goal)
Fast forward to high school and my ideas kept evolving...
Tenth Grade: Attend college and go into journalism (getting warmer now!)
Eleventh Grade: Further my education and be happy

The same day that I looked through this memory book I was dismayed to read an article on what some of today's children are hoping to achieve in the future. Lego, a brand that may have brought you much joy as a child, was curious to learn about the career aspirations of today's generation. In honor of the fiftieth anniversary of Neil Armstrong's historic walk on the moon in 1969, the company conducted a poll of three thousand children aged eight to twelve from the United States, the United Kingdom, and China. The children could choose among the professions of astronaut, musician, professional athlete, teacher, or vlogger/YouTuber. The number one choice among American and British youngsters was vlogger/YouTuber, while the majority of Chinese children selected astronaut.[1]

We can set an example for the children in our culture who would rather broadcast amateur videos of themselves on YouTube than voyage to another planet. The first way is clear cut and the running theme of this book: put down your own phone and restrict or eliminate their access. The second way is to revisit the goals, however lofty, that we set for ourselves in our idealistic youth. This doesn't mean that if you wanted to be a rock star when you were thirteen that you're going to quit your job and assemble a band in your garage. Rather, reacquainting yourself with the dream could mean signing up for a guitar lesson, buying tickets for a local concert, or just singing karaoke in the living room.

The dreams and interests we cherished as children bridge the distance between who we are now and who we are meant to be. Though it may not be probable to paint seascapes and pay the mortgage, we can carve out free time for such cathartic pursuits. You may not be a professional NBA player, but you can shoot hoops in the driveway instead of staying indoors on the phone. I might rather write historical fiction than pound out technical articles, but I can revisit my writing passion when the sun goes down.

Time Well Spent

Enjoying our free time, truly enjoying it, is a goal that many of us don't take seriously enough. Our to-do lists are longer every day, often because we compromise them by wasting time online. Even if you spend just one hour per day in leisure online, that hour becomes seven spread across a week, which then creeps towards an entire work day. The four-day work week has yet to gain a foothold in the United States, though it's already the norm in the Netherlands where employees average twenty-nine combined hours in the office Tuesday through Friday. Though the four-day work week is not standard for American companies, the idea is appealing to many employees who feel that their jobs leave them little time to unwind. (Remember the "Sunday Scaries" we talked about?) If we covet a four-day work week, then why would we essentially engage in a six-day work week by casting away one hour per day on the phone? Phones are miniature computers, after all, and I don't think most of us would want

FLORA HOPE LONDON, M.A.

to stare at a desktop version for an extra hour each day. So, why do we make exceptions with our phones?

We have convinced ourselves that scrolling is relaxing and a contemporary form of leisure. But have you ever felt *better* after an hour on your phone the way you would after the same amount of time in, say, a park? We're not sipping umbrella drinks in the tropics when we are on our phones, though we might be fixating over photos of our "friends" in their vacation lounge chairs, which only creates a beast of virtual envy. Watching others check items off their bucket lists does nothing to help us emulate this proactive behavior and instead arouses the ugliness of envy. This envy can also morph into depression, as studies demonstrate how social media and the Internet in general lower self-esteem. Thus, a vicious cycle sets into motion: Waste time on phone – get depressed – waste more time on phone – get more depressed – accomplish nothing.

Offline Solution #23: *Do you consider your phone a form of entertainment? Look at your phone from a new perspective as you brainstorm five enjoyable past-times that don't require technology. Perhaps the past-times will be linked to the insightful career ideas you nurtured as a child.*

THEN THERE ARE the more substantial goals that we don't have time or energy to chase. Maybe you don't just want to paint those seascapes but you want to show them in a gallery and sell them to art collectors. Playing basketball informally is fun, but perhaps you endeavor to coach a team of young people in your community. And I don't just want to dabble in historical fiction; I want to write a novel worthy of a wide readership and...maybe the Pulitzer Prize? As long as we're setting goals here, there should be no limitations to what we aspire to achieve. Why, then, do our goals so often tease us in the untouchable distance, never to be achieved? Stress management consultant and mindfulness expert Patrizia Collard, Ph.D. has a theory.

> ...we procrastinate in our lives. We avoid engaging with the real thing – our life – because subconsciously we want to avoid failing and being alone. So, instead of pursuing something worthwhile and meaningful, we keep writing emails, texting or phoning anybody who comes to mind. If we never finish this 'project,' you see, it can never fail.[2]

An unfinished project can also never succeed and we are often as afraid of professional and personal victory as we are of failure. If we succeed at an endeavor, then suddenly we have attained a higher level and the fall could be steep. In that way, even a hesitation to succeed is akin to a fear of failing. We also may wonder if we deserve success or if we are frauds reaching for castles in the sky. It would be much easier to download another game app and "succeed" at something more inconsequential. As spiritual writer and 2020 presidential candidate Marianne Williamson expresses in these oft quoted lines from her book, *A Return to Love:*

> Our deepest fear is not that we are inadequate. Our deepest fear is that we are powerful beyond measure. It is our light, not our darkness that most frightens us.[3]

There is a man in my local writer's group who exemplifies this fear of being extraordinary, or inadequate, depending on your perspective. Last week, Rachid was working on an anthology of contemporary political essays. This week he's drafting a critical analysis on the works of early 20th century poet William Butler Yeats. His project from a few months ago, a dystopian science fiction novel, never made it past the first chapter. Rachid's mind is bursting with brilliant ideas and he has the makings of a prolific writer – if only he would focus on one goal and see it through to completion. And yes of course, Rachid checks his phone every few minutes during our weekly meetings.

Whether your personal fear is failure or success – or if by chance you're feeling fearless – now is the best time to unearth that buried project. Now is the best time to shut the phone off and tackle that painting, report, repair, recipe, novel – whatever it is that you have been avoiding through the mask of your phone. Our phones make procrastination enticing; it's so tempting to discard the difficult work of worthwhile goals and fall into the trap of mindlessness.

We have discussed at length how smart devices, and the Internet as a whole, fragment our attention. Therefore, you should expect an uphill climb if you finally resolve to accomplish that distant goal. There were many days when I was writing this book that I had to force myself to sit down and concentrate. As American poet Dorothy Parker memorably said, "Writing is the art of applying the ass to the seat." The same is true of any goal we aspire to achieve. Shortcuts or avoidance will try to call us away from the intense work that is the only legitimate path to a goal.

Even though my phone is long gone, I have found that the tendency towards distraction has remained. My phone had conditioned me to expect everything to be instantly available, ready with one light tap of the index finger. In stark contrast, writing a book or pursuing any major goal is a marathon when we would like it to be a sprint. Think of Michelangelo who painted the Sistine Chapel over an arduous period of four years from 1508 to 1512. Michelangelo and his team of assistants naturally grew tired of working on the same painstakingly detailed paintings day after day, year after year.

In fact, Michelangelo wrote a poem in 1509, just one year into the quest, on his abject misery from the physical strain of intricately decorating the ceiling of a building hailed as sacred.[4] Then he carried on with his meaningful work. What if Michelangelo and his team had given up and slammed their paintbrushes onto the floor in a fit of frustration? What if they had walked away from this monumental undertaking and decided that it was just too hard? Art, architecture, and history would each be poorer without the dedication that Michelangelo poured into his iconic frescoes. We have the power to create smaller scale masterpieces when we simply focus.

Happy & Healthy

A peculiar word – hygge – has entered the global consciousness. The Danish term (pronounced HOO-gah) doesn't have a direct translation into English, but the concept is easily illustrated. In the winter, you bundle up with a downy soft fleece throw and a steaming mug of spiced apple cider. You wear feet pajamas to bed even though you feel ridiculous in them and you light a candle in every window for passersby to admire. Hygge is comfort food for the soul, a cozy mode of living that is designed for the colder months but can be channeled any time of year.

The idea gained widespread attention in 2016 when the World Happiness Report ranked Denmark the number one happiest country in the world for the third time.[5] With dozens of hygge books now published, you can reap the warm, fuzzy rewards whether you live in Copenhagen or

Copacabana. The catch? You'll need to put down the phone. Although Denmark has one of the highest smartphone penetration rates in the world, by some counts even higher than that of the United States, the Danes aren't using their devices when they're wrapped up in their hygge blankets. Smartphones and hygge are like peanut butter and sardines, according to experts in the cultural tradition. This excerpt from an article about the pleasures of hygge and camping makes it clear how smartphones are not part of the gear we should be packing.

> A major component to hygge has always been being present, long before smartphones were stealing our attention. The Danish believe the good, simple things in life must be savored and enjoyed. So, set the phone aside for the day and take note of the sights, smells, and sounds of your campsite. Exchange stories and laughter with your camp crew without scrolling through your Twitter feed. Or spend the afternoon by yourself getting consumed in a nurturing activity like painting, knitting, writing, or reading a good book in a hammock.[6]

This camping trip sounds a lot like Catalina Island transported to the woods. Again, we may escape our stressful devices temporarily during such an excursion, but what happens when we come home? We scroll through our phones and eat take-out pizza.

You have a choice: take home a box of crispy brick oven pizza or make the pie from scratch. Most busy people will choose the first option. I was certainly opting for the take-out pizza, sushi, and sandwiches almost every day when I owned a smartphone. The phone had made me lazy and complacent in every area of my life, including the kitchen. Post-smartphone, I was inspired to break out the stainless steel cookware and make easy dishes like ratatouille over basmati rice. Over time my culinary skills became more complex as my patience grew in tandem with my upgraded lifestyle. Preparing a loaf of chocolate banana walnut bread on a Sunday morning became a weekly event. Home cooking, by the way, is another way to practice the happy art of hygge.

Plus, there is no question that home cooking is healthier than dining at restaurants or shoving a plastic tray of chemical goop into the microwave. Living without the smartphone elucidated why I had resorted to the latter for so many years. Tuning out the world on my device meant that I was also ignoring my body's basic need for real sustenance. I learned that cooking correlated to a newfound respect for my whole wellbeing: body, mind and spirit. Picture a typical dinner in your household. If a time crunch is the norm, would it be less of an issue if you put down the phone for an extra thirty minutes in the evening?

The Mindful Component

Healthy self-esteem causes us to treat our bodies like temples rather than garbage disposals. We should afford our minds the same respectful or even reverent handling. When we start our day with a rundown of sleazy news stories, we are most definitely relegating our minds to garbage disposal status. The effects can be both damaging and lasting. The more we feed our minds trash, the more we will do the same with our bodies. Everything is out of synch at once because everything is complementary and it is not possible to have a healthy body without a nourished mind.

Diets fail for many reasons, but one overlooked reason may be the mind-body connection. Plowing through a liquid fast is a quick way to burn off a handful of pounds in a week, but we know that it is not sustainable. Changing habits, cooking from scratch, devoting thirty minutes a day to moderate exercise, making those recommended eight hours of sleep a priority – these are the keys to long-term weight loss maintenance. Mind and body will be in balance with a conscientious lifestyle. Similarly, our minds and bodies will unite in overall health when we peel away the toxic layers. For me, the smartphone was the most poisonous, so I removed it completely and healed more thoroughly than I would have thought possible.

Sadly, too many of us are doing the exact opposite. The *Washington Post* has reported that some young people are developing hornlike structures or bone spurs at the backs of their skulls. A group of researchers from the University of the Sunshine Coast in Queensland, Australia, attribute the unusual growths to a sustained forward tilt of the head that occurs when people are using their phones. Other scientists disagree and believe that the bone spurs may have other less grim explanations while still others argue that the protrusions may be an optical illusion.[7]

When I was eighteen, I visited a podiatrist to treat chronic blisters on my feet that were making it painful to walk. With a sick fascination, the doctor stared at my protruding bone spurs and curling toes and proclaimed, "You have the worst feet I have ever seen in twenty-two years of practicing medicine. You have the feet of an eighty-year-old woman! Could you walk for me a little?"

Mortified, I took a few halting steps forward as he let out a low whistle and chuckled at how my feet were "almost completely flat. I mean, there's no arch at all." He gleefully continued, "You're going to have to use orthotic inserts for the rest of your life and eventually get surgery – a bunionectomy. The bone spurs will probably get worse too…" As the podiatrist rambled on, I wondered if those orthotic inserts would fit into my favorite pair of summer white stilettos. Surgery was too terrible for my teenage mind to contemplate, so I scowled in protest at the doctor's framed diploma on the wall.

Since that humiliating appointment, my feet have never ceased to cause me distress. They are literally my Achilles' heel. I have endured subsequent lower back problems for more than twenty years from the misalignment of the bones in my feet. When my back goes out, the pain can last for weeks and be so searing that I am unable to sit down.

The point of this story is to illustrate that bone spurs are no laughing matter despite the cultural jokes that have circulated about draft dodgers. If young people are developing these extra bones *in the backs of their skulls*, there are likely to be consequences much later on. For now, those consequences remain a mystery as the smartphone is too recent of an invention for history to guide us. Again, some sources have also called the study into question and challenged the scientific methods used. But even if the study is completely debunked, it is not difficult to see how smartphones can affect the musculoskeletal system. Slumped shoulders and a bowed head wreak havoc on spinal alignment and can lead to the same kinds of back problems as misshapen feet. We already know this from spending too much time at our desks, thus the proliferation of standing work stations. Further, text neck and cellphone elbow are two painful conditions already established to bear a connection with digital technology. Also referred to as "digital disabilities," these repetitive strain injuries are linked to handheld devices.[8]

Healing Our Bodies and Minds Together

How can we combat these common injuries? Yoga is a pleasant remedy for more than 20 million Americans who practice the discipline. To address my back problems without the aid of prescription medication, I began studying yoga when I was twenty-six. Since then I have participated in thousands of classes in the United States and abroad along with earning a teaching certification. No matter where I have practiced yoga, whether in downtown San Diego or a mountain village in Costa Rica, there is one common denominator: people make a beeline for the door during the most important part of class.

Most yoga instructors will tell you that yoga nidra is the most vital portion of the entire sixty to ninety minute class. During these final minutes, students recline on their mats, close their eyes, and drift into meditation. After an hour or more of conscious breathing and full body stretches, one would think that yoga nidra would be a natural culmination. Not so for the gaggle of students noisily gathering up their car keys and cell phones as the slow rhythm of a Djembe drum pulsates through the speakers at the twilight of every class. Their rubber soled shoes invariably squeak as they charge to the exit while the few of us who remain attempt to ignore them. Maybe they have somewhere to go or maybe they can't sit still for one second longer and would rather trample their fellow classmates. The fear of being alone with our thoughts resurges. Silence, whether inner or outer, is such a rare occurrence that we don't know how to handle it, so we bolt out the door whether literal or figurative. If only we could do as Depeche Mode sang in 1990 – enjoy the silence – our minds and bodies might synchronize.

Offline Solution #24: *If chanting "om" while sitting in lotus pose isn't your cup of tea, there are other forms of exercise that can help you realign. Pilates tones not only the abdominal muscles but the entire core, including thighs, buttocks and lower back, which all* *work together to support the spine. Tai Chi is a gentle martial art that emphasizes good posture as well as precision of movement. Qigong is a related discipline that is believed to cultivate energy through flowing movements and controlled breathing. Any of these mind-body workouts can be performed in the comfort of your home, or better yet, outdoors to capture the full meditative essence.*

THE GOLDEN EGG

**"The present is the ever moving shadow that divides
yesterday from tomorrow. In that lies hope."
- Frank Lloyd Wright**

ABOUT TEN YEARS AGO, my writing career was in a state of
flux, or more accurately, a state of disaster. Paying the rent
late made eviction a growing threat and eating strawberry
toaster pastries for dinner a nightly routine. That year I was
invited to Christmas brunch with my extended family, a
brood which included about a dozen aunts and uncles plus
countless cousins. Rather than do something smart and frugal
like Secret Santa, my family decided that everyone should
receive a gift from *everyone*. Shopping at pricey department
stores or even big box stores was not an option for me, so I
sauntered into the dollar store with my chin held high.

I purchased twenty-five calendars at one dollar each and

wrapped them in gift paper that I had also snagged for a buck. *Nobody will know the difference,* I told myself as I loaded my car up on a snowy northern Christmas morning and drove to my aunt's swanky suburban home. After a brunch of poached eggs, buttermilk pancakes, and frosty mimosas, we sat down by the tree to unveil the gifts. At first, no one blinked an eye when they unwrapped my calendars. That is, not until one curious preteen cousin removed the protective shrink wrap, sliding the flimsy calendar out as the thin pages ripped and practically disintegrated in his hands. He burst out in contagious laughter and soon the whole room was guffawing at my expense.

I sighed. My dollar store scheme had backfired and left me looking like a cheapskate and a fool. It would have been much better if I had taken the time to design homemade calendars with family photographs instead of stockpiling generic junk. I imagined that mocking laughter transforming into warm smiles as my relatives flipped through pages of happy memories, enough pages to fill an entire year. Too late I realized that time is the greatest gift we have to offer and it has no price tag, astronomical or bargain basement.

Time is the golden egg that hatches when we nurture it with our most earnest efforts. Pursuing a goal to completion, nourishing our bodies with home cooked goodness, and communing with nature are all ways to ensure that golden egg doesn't transmute into rust before we hatch it. Laure Dugas, wine connoisseur and author of the memoir, *Champagne Baby: How One Parisian Learned to Love Wine – and Life – the American Way,* manifests this concept in these metaphorical lines:

Drinking wine is a string of moments. Each sip is discrete – you lift the glass, allow the wine to infiltrate your nose and run over your tongue, and put the glass down again – but most people will remember it as one continuous experience, unless they're really paying attention. If you don't notice each moment, they blur, rather than connect, and instead of a braid of pleasures and observations, you are left only with a fuzzy memory. You remember you did *something* – but not what it felt like to do it.

It's the same with life. The years go by like *that*. If you don't pay attention to everything you see and do, every nerve tingling, every firing synapse, then the experience cannot touch you. You are cutting off your memories before they even have a chance to form.[1]

To compare wine, one of life's finer pleasures, to the ordinary moments of our days, is nothing less than magnificent. We don't gulp down a glass of wine like we chug a can of soda, and we shouldn't amass a whiplash collection of moments filtered through screens and artificial lighting like a demented cartoon. One high quality square of dark chocolate is infinitely more delectable than a whole corn syrup-laden candy bar. One picture perfect moment cherished in our memories is better than dozens of stilted photos taken for public consumption. One brilliant book that keeps you eagerly turning the pages is more pleasurable than a hundred bad news blurbs that make you want to hide under the bed. One minute embracing a pet is sweeter than endless hours cradling a phone. One hour devoted to accomplishing a goal is superior to ten minutes of spying on social media.

Mindfulness is not a buzz word; it is a blueprint for how to live our fullest lives. The mindless lethargy of smartphone usage obliterates any attempts at mindfulness and thus at a wholly engaged life. Sometimes we do need a respite from reality, but daydreaming not disconnecting is the antidote.

Daydreaming leads to brainstorming and brainstorming leads to brilliant ideas. Sports and leisure activities serve us as well, but online gaming and scrolling only lead us further away from the refreshment we so desperately need. An hour of forest bathing invigorates us while half that time online depletes us. Even if we live a three-hour drive from the nearest forest, we can make one major change and reward ourselves with instant yet enduring invigoration.

As I was conducting research for this book, I came across an Internet slang term that was new to me: JOMO. The joy of missing out is the antithesis of the fear of missing out. Those of us who live the majority of our lives offline already understand the sacredness of JOMO and the irony that we are not missing out on anything at all when our computer screens go dark. Quite the opposite, we are gaining everything.

Starlight

Sometimes I feel like I am mourning the loss of my friends to the digital cosmos, including two Generation X gal pals, one who has admitted to "liking" photos on Instagram while we're talking on the phone and another who hasn't called me since 2011. The latter friend relies solely on email communication to keep our friendship afloat. Email was adequate if unsatisfying when we lived forty minutes apart and frequently met for lunch, but since I have moved more than 1,200 miles away, those messages need a more personal upgrade.

Offline Solution #25: *Call a friend whose voice you haven't heard in years. Maybe you've been "in touch" through social media or email, but you haven't truly connected. Surprise that friend with an old-fashioned phone call and set a date for your next one!*

OFTEN I FEEL ALONE in my choice to reclaim my life, like an anachronism or a relic from another century – even another millennium. Perhaps this is how a 21st century pop star might feel belting out a medieval fugue when everyone else is warbling along with Auto-Tune. Be prepared for some gape-mouthed paralysis if you decide to cross the mountain to offline rebellion. Awkward silence often followed my announcements as people acted like I had just told them that I sleep on a splintered floorboard in a dungeon from the Dark Ages. Even people who were decades older than me couldn't understand why I thought life was actually better *without* a smartphone being the Apple of my eye. Wasn't it supposed to be the other way around, that smartphones make life better? It's all a matter of perspective: one person may see me as a cavewoman while another might consider me a trailblazer. But I am aware that the majority of people probably view me as the former. Fortunately, the Wilma Flintstone in me doesn't mind at all.

My reaction to the criticism, judgments, and painful spells of silence has been to persevere. If my decision is getting under people's skin, then it must be revolutionary. Either that or people take their devices a little too personally.

Finally, I should note that despite all the bashing throughout this book, I believe the smartphone and its smart offspring are brilliant innovations. But then again, so was the atomic bomb. I can't help but hear REM's "It's the End of the World as We Know It," whenever I think of either of those earth tilting inventions.

Admittedly, though, there have been instances when I have wished that I had a mobile phone. Last night a hammering thunderstorm struck the Gulf Coast and knocked out the electricity for a few hours. I was shocked when I picked up my landline to make a call and there was no dial tone. My Wi-Fi connection was also dead in the water. I recalled the exciting thunderstorms of my youth when a power outage had no correlation with the telephone plugged into the wall. *How everything has changed*, I thought. There I was, alone in the dark with no connection to civilization, much like I was on the country road inches away from that mysterious ditch.

Was I frightened? At first I was a bit unnerved, then I was relieved. The lights that keep my apartment complex shining even at 3 am were out of commission. There was no flicker of a television through a neighbor's window and no noise from someone's home movie and popcorn night. The hours felt primitive and peaceful in a way that is no longer possible except in the unusual event of electrical failure.

I have not glimpsed a star in the sky since I was a child. Widespread urban and suburban light pollution have turned our skies dark and hazy and obscured the enchantment of starlight. Van Gogh's "Starry Night" may have been called "Starless Night" if he had painted it in the 21st century rather than the nineteenth. As rain pelted the windowpanes, I looked out into the blackness and thought I saw the glimmer of a star or two winking at me that they were still there.

Your Light

The word *rebel* has sharp undercurrents of violence and struggle. But what I am really doing with my life, and have hopefully helped you to do with yours, is to make peace. Living 1,000 percent in the moment ushers in peace; connecting with loved ones brings peace; daydreaming away an afternoon in a green space fosters peace – and maybe even a dazzling idea that will change the course of our lives.

For these reasons and more, I will not purchase another soul-sucking smartphone. I will continue to enjoy my life as a peaceful offline rebel, paving the way with my story for others to write their own. No matter what shiny new gadgets crowd out the smartphone on the market, I don't want to own any of them. And certainly none of them will ever own me again. One single device, my laptop computer, is sufficient for me to navigate the digital world. All other devices are superfluous. Because frankly I'm smart enough. And so are you. I apply this self-sufficient attitude to all technology, viewing it as a tool and a means to an end, not a destination in itself.

Rootedness in the present moment is non-negotiable to our well-being. Speeding through life with our body heat fogging up the glass screens in our palms does not nurture our well-being. If we were meant to live in the future-oriented fast lane, the term would be well-becoming, not well-being.

We are the architects of our own lives. We build peace from the inside out, beginning with reflection on our true needs and desires: companionship, tranquility, purpose, creativity, nature. Once we have sketched a canvas of inner peace, we fine-tune our reactions to the world around us: smiling at that not-so-scary stranger; dropping everything when our best friend of twenty years is in crisis; paying attention to the wondrousness of the clouds floating across a turquoise sky.

To be this kind of revolutionary peacemaker, we need to be free of hindrances, including the one fused to our hip like an alien appendage. We need to take the phrase "fully present" to a higher level, understanding that the greatest gift we can ever give others, or ourselves, is presence. Physical presence is only the beginning. Emotional, intellectual, and spiritual presence follow when we are attuned to *real* reality rather than the virtual imitation. The natural result of this multi-layered presence is a life well-lived. Conscious moments become vivid memories and the living proof that we have hatched all our golden eggs.

Being offline means being on and lit up for magic. When the blue lights of our smartphones extinguish, our inner lights spark to vibrant life.

III

LIVE YOUR MAGIC

"Whatever you can do, or dream you can, begin it. Boldness
has genius, power, and magic in it."
- W.H. Murray

13

TOP 10 BENEFITS OF LIVING WITHOUT A SMARTPHONE

1. You'll feel better physically and may have fewer aches and pains.
2. You'll feel clearer mentally and your focus will improve.
3. You'll set boundaries and protect your free time.
4. You'll have more energy for social activities and creative projects.
5. Your loved ones will thank you.
6. You just might sleep like a baby.
7. Your privacy won't be under 24/7 attack.
8. People will admire your willpower and individualism. They might even be inspired to follow your lead.
9. The little BIG moments that give life meaning will no longer pass you by.
10. Life will simply be more magical.

14

THE OFFLINE REBEL THREE-WEEK ACTION PLAN

IT's time to turbocharge ideas into action! In this 21-day plan, we'll revisit the offline tools explored throughout the book and apply them into our everyday lives step by step.

Each week includes daily guidelines that you can tweak to fit your lifestyle and personality. At the end of each week is a Weekly Challenge which calls on you to do something completely out of the box.

Finally, you might be ready for The Ultimate Challenge which is where that Boldness IQ will come in handy!

By the end of twenty-one days, the goal is for you to be happily smartphone-free. But this is a personalized plan and it's *your* journey, so you may decide to keep the smartphone and simply use it less (hopefully a LOT less).

You can expect these three weeks to be simultaneously challenging and liberating. Keep an open mind as you journal your impressions and decrease your smartphone usage in ways that may feel uncomfortable at first. Discomfort is an indication that major change is on the way.

Grab a journal & pencil and let the offline rebellion begin!

~

Week One:

Assess & Reduce

As you begin this three-week action plan, it is vital to be honest and accurate about your smartphone usage. You may be shocked by how much time you actually spend on your phone. Whatever your starting point is, you'll gradually reduce your smartphone usage throughout this first week, becoming less dependent on the device and less compulsive about checking it. Think of these first seven days as preparation for much more dramatic changes still to come.

Day 1

Download an app that measures the exact amount of time you spend on your smartphone and record the number. How would you like that number to change at the end of three weeks? Set your specific goal now.

Day 2

Turn your smartphone off for one full hour. Keep the phone out of sight if possible (the bottom of a sock drawer is an ideal place!) How did you feel during this hour without your phone? Nervous? Relieved? Impatient?

Day 3

Again, turn your smartphone off for one full hour. Notice any differences in how you feel today. Did the hour pass more quickly? Did you want to keep the phone off for more than an hour? Or was this exercise difficult?

Day 4

Today we're shutting the phone off for two full hours. During that time, think of a hobby that you have neglected.

Gardening? Jogging? Painting? Spend at least an hour of your offline time rediscovering that hobby. If it's a work day, set aside an hour in the evening and take back this quality time with yourself and one of your passions.

Day 5

Decide how long you want your phone to be turned off today. If it's just fifteen minutes, then let it be. If it's all day, then let it be. Start to develop the healthy habit of designating an offline chunk of time every day. What did you do while your phone was off? Were you more productive? Relaxed? How did you feel when you turned the phone back on?

Day 6

As we near the end of the first week, you have hopefully become accustomed to honoring an offline period each day. If you have, try to increase the amount of time your phone is powered down. If you haven't, then continue to turn the device off for at least fifteen minutes no matter what.

In addition to your designated offline time, notice when you reach for your phone throughout the day. Are you bored when you want to check your phone? Stressed? Worried about missing something? Every time you want to reach for your phone, take three deep, conscious breaths and turn your attention elsewhere. If you can, step outside and take a five-minute stroll. Reevaluate how you feel and if you still want to grab the phone.

Day 7

Time assessment day! Use your app to measure the exact amount of time you spend on your smartphone today and record the number.

How does it compare to the time you spent on Day 1? How close or far are you from your goal?

To help you steadily decrease your screen time, disable notifications for all but your most important contacts. Ignore non-urgent messages and respond only to those that need immediate attention. Likewise, refrain from sending any unnecessary messages to others. Does this approach give you more time in the day? Do you think it would be beneficial to reduce how much time you spend texting? How so?

Weekly Challenge

Count how many apps you have on your smartphone. Take inventory of their importance (or uselessness) and rank them. Delete the bottom half of your ranking list. Just like that. Make a pact with yourself not to download any additional apps for the next two weeks.

Week Two:

Dive into Enjoyment

THIS WEEK you'll widen the bridge between your online and offline time. You'll experience your offline moments more fully as you spend even less time with the smartphone than you did in Week 1. Get ready to leave the smartphone behind and go full steam ahead with your real life!

Day 8

Venture out without your smartphone. Go to a park, a café, a bookstore, any place you choose. How does it feel to be in public without your smartphone? Do you find yourself reaching for it? What do you observe about other people and their smartphone usage in public?

Day 9

When you wake up this morning, do anything but check your smartphone. For the first hour of the day, eat breakfast, work out, read, journal – do absolutely anything but scroll through your device.

Day 10

Stop checking your smartphone at least one hour before you go to bed tonight. Devote the last hour of your day to something worthwhile, whether it's talking with the members of your household, spending uninterrupted time with your pet, or reading a book.

Day 11

Combine Days 9 and 10 – not checking your smartphone first thing in the morning or last thing in the evening. Reclaim those two hours for yourself and your health. How do you feel? Have you noticed any changes in your sleep patterns? Has it been easy or challenging to ignore the smartphone in the morning and evening?

Day 12

Look through your list of contacts and identify your closest friends. Choose one or two. If you usually text these friends, surprise them with the sound of your voice today. If they took your call, how was the conversation different from your texting chats? If they didn't take the call, how did it make you feel?

Day 13

Do you check your phone at work? Or perhaps the better question is: how often do you check your phone at work and does it interfere with your job performance? Commit to only checking your phone three times during the workday: when you arrive, at lunch, and when you leave. What changes do you notice in your work habits and productivity? Are you more engaged with co-workers and/or clients?

Day 14

Increase the amount of time you wait before checking your phone in the morning and turning it off at night. Go for two hours each instead of one. Do you notice yourself becoming more alert in the morning and more easeful at night? What has been replacing these hours that might have been spent on your smartphone? Do you feel ready to go longer without the device?

Weekly Challenge

Pick a free date and commit to it on your calendar. Then, plan a day trip which will keep you away from home for at least six hours. You know what's coming next...leave the smartphone in the sock drawer.

Week Three:

Carve out Deep Calm

HERE WE ARE in the final week of this action plan and the beginning of a richer quality of life for you and all those you love. At this threshold, it's time to make a big decision: are you going to live without your smartphone or just live with less of it? Either way you are making a wise decision for your life. But we still have one more week to flow through, so let's go! The Ultimate Challenge awaits...

Day 15

Start creating your bedroom sanctuary. Make the room a more relaxing place with touches like accent pillows, aromatherapy candles, and live plants. Tonight, don't just stop looking at your phone an hour before sleep but relegate it to the farthest corner of your bedroom until morning.

Day 16

Give your smartphone the boot tonight and leave it in the bathroom, living room, or any other separate space that works for you. How was your sleep impacted? Did it make you edgy or calm to have the phone far away?

Day 17

Evaluate your new level of control over your phone. Approximately how many times a day are you checking the smartphone now as we move towards the pinnacle of this journey? How much time are you spending on the phone overall? Check in again with your Day 1 goal.

Day 18

If you haven't already, share your progress with the special people in your life. Notice their reactions. Some may be taken aback and skeptical while others will probably want to give this peaceful lifestyle a whirl. Experience their reactions without judgment and carry on with your personal voyage.

Day 19

Reevaluate the apps you have on your phone. You already slashed the number in half at the end of Week 1, so see if you might be able to halve the remaining apps. You might like to scour the phone for any apps that could be used for entertainment purposes and let them go. Notice how your relationship with the phone evolves as you view it exclusively as a practical tool.

Day 20

Take back meal time! If you use your phone during meals, whether at home, at work, or at a restaurant, start breaking the cycle. Eat your food more slowly and pay attention to how much you eat and when you feel full. Try not to replace the smartphone with another distraction, like a magazine or newspaper.

Day 21

Prepare for the Weekly Challenge by checking your smartphone only once every four hours today – or even less frequently if you're so inspired.

Weekly Challenge

Designate a 100 percent tech-free day, shutting down not

only your smartphone but all digital devices for twenty-four hours. How did you spend the time? Did you cheat? Imagine how it would feel to spend an entire weekend or even a vacation without digital distractions. Journey through your thoughts and turn them into action if you dare...

THE ULTIMATE CHALLENGE

YOUR FINAL CHALLENGE is not just for Week Three but possibly for the long-term. Here it is: get rid of your smartphone. Sell it if you own it. Return it if it's on lease. Trade it in for a basic phone or hook up a landline. Unshackle yourself from the chains of mobile cyberspace and grab a spoon to start stirring up that bold magic.

If you accept this challenge (or even reduce your time online) then I will have done my job as an author. In the words of Thoreau, "A truly good book teaches me better than to read it. I must soon lay it down, and commence living on its hint. What I began by reading, I must finish by acting."

So, do you accept The Ultimate Challenge? Why or why not? If not, do you think you might accept it at some point in the future? Will you accept this challenge with other forms of technology or, on a larger scale, anything which detracts from your quality of life or compromises your freedom and privacy?

Maybe you feel that a smartphone enhances your quality of life and feeds your freedom which is understandable – and the prevailing perspective nowadays. But if you do decide to accept The Ultimate Challenge, you'll be in very successful company. Billionaire investor Warren Buffett reportedly owns an iPhone X but has yet to set it up. Instead, Buffett relies on a much more basic offline model that sells for as little as $20 on eBay. At a business luncheon in 2019 Buffett joked, "Here's my phone, incidentally. Alexander Graham Bell lent it to me and I forgot to return it."[1]

Like Buffett, you might have the last laugh when you're breezing through your days with no notifications, relaxation turned on, stress powered down.

100 FUN & CREATIVE OFFLINE IDEAS

1. Take a walk or jog in the fresh air and sunshine
2. Meet your best friend for coffee, scones, and phone-free conversation
3. Read a novel in a juicy genre: fantasy, romance, sci fi, mystery, thriller
4. Take an old-fashioned photography class and print out your creations
5. Go on a bike ride and explore local park trails
6. Journal your thoughts first thing in the morning
7. Paint and decorate your favorite coffee mug or teacup
8. Go out dancing with your partner or friends
9. Plant a tree or patch of garden in your community
10. Indulge in buttered popcorn and a double feature at the movie theater
11. Visit your public library and borrow some books
12. Take a day trip and pack a picnic lunch
13. Host a pot luck dinner party and make it a trivia night
14. Redecorate your home with fresh artwork and accents

15. Attend a poetry slam and listen...or sign up to read your work

16. Bake a cake from scratch even if it's nobody's birthday

17. Look for free yoga and meditation classes and try one out

18. Revamp your resume and take the plunge into a career change

19. Call an old friend who you haven't spoken with in years

20. Write a funny or nostalgic memoir about your youth

21. Pick up that musical instrument you haven't touched since 6th grade

22. Play board games with your family or friends

23. Do spring cleaning even if it's the middle of autumn

24. Go to an art supply store and channel your inner O'Keefe

25. Check out a real O'Keefe at a museum and imagine the painter's thoughts

26. Join an adult volleyball or softball league

27. Attend a language class at a community college and brush up on your Spanish

28. Make your own holiday cards to snail mail this season

29. Take a train ride or river cruise and disappear for an afternoon

30. Volunteer at an animal shelter, soup kitchen, or anywhere that warms your heart

31. Brainstorm side business ideas and set one into motion

32. Spend more quality time with...(you fill in the blank)

33. Try the new restaurant that just opened up in town

34. Walk and window shop through a mall on a rainy day

35. Experiment with recipes from different cultural cuisines

36. Start a woodworking or home improvement project

37. Purge unneeded belongings and donate to your choice of charity

38. Go out for ice cream cones after an ordinary dinner at home

39. Gaze at the night sky and see how many stars you can count

40. Hike, snowshoe, kayak, or embark on some other outdoor adventure

41. Play with your kids and/or your pets

42. Turn up the music and mop the floors with a dip and a twist

43. Rediscover a comic book you loved as a kid

44. Attend a local networking event and learn your neighbors' names

45. Shut the blinds and take a well-deserved nap

46. Light candles and set a romantic mood...

47. Go to a busy public place and engage in the lost art of people watching

48. Write a friendly letter and hand-deliver it to someone in a nursing home

49. Take a tour of a historic site in your area and be a student without homework

50. Write a budget and tack it on the refrigerator to help you reach your goals

51. Go totally off the grid on a camping trip – don't forget the marshmallows!

52. Read the Sunday paper over a cappuccino and muffin

53. Tease your brain with a crossword puzzle, number game, or optical illusion

54. Take a stroll through your neighborhood and note the new details you discover

55. Dare to participate in Improv Night at a comedy club

56. Start a bedtime ritual: hot tea, breathing exercises, inspirational readings

57. Go to a roller rink or trampoline zone to skate/jump through your stress

58. Play charades and laugh until you cry at your next party

59. Schedule a pampering spa or beauty service or DIY at home
60. Browse at neighborhood garage and antiques sales
61. Stock up on seasonal treats like summer watermelon or winter chestnuts
62. Explore the offline features of your computer – write a story!
63. Visit a farm sanctuary and pet the animals
64. Belt out karaoke like nobody's listening and you have the voice of an angel
65. Try something that scares you – Ziplining? Tree climbing? Conquer your fear!
66. Visit a nature center and learn about the flora and fauna
67. Spend a hot day lounging at the beach or pool
68. Find a pick-your-own orchard and get a new perspective on the food you eat
69. Snag concert tickets and experience the thrill of live music
70. Reconnect with a neglected hobby – golf, scrapbooking, ceramics, you name it
71. Play retro arcade games like pinball and Pac-Man
72. Set up a scavenger hunt in your backyard
73. Start that project you've been putting off – and don't stop until it's finished
74. Print out photos of happy memories, frame them, and hang them on the walls
75. Go to a bookstore and buy a book on a subject you know nothing about
76. Wake up early to watch the sunrise
77. Sleep in on the weekend and eat Belgian waffles in bed
78. Learn a new skill: horseback riding, acting, belly dancing – the sky's the limit
79. Run through the rain and hope for a rainbow
80. Write a thank-you note to an old teacher or coach and send it

81. Get crafty with homemade soap, candles, potpourri sachets

82. Stay outside past sunset on a beautiful day

83. Go for a joy ride with the windows down and radio pumping

84. Compile a cookbook of traditional family recipes & distribute copies to relatives

85. Surprise a loved one with a bouquet of flowers "just because"

86. Talk to people on line (not online!) at the café or grocery store

87. Decorate a plain T-shirt with a bold message of motivation

88. Sketch out a family tree for posterity

89. Attend a town hall meeting and speak your mind about an important issue

90. Create a vision board from magazine clippings and natural materials

91. Challenge a friend to a silly session of Mad Libs

92. Buy a science kit for your kid (or yourself) and feel the joy of discovery

93. Throw a paint party and spruce up those dull walls or cabinets

94. Plant your own herb or vegetable garden and skip the supermarket

95. Decompress with an adult coloring book and freshly sharpened set of pencils

96. Make your own calendar from your favorite photos of people and places

97. Taste test different brands of delicious foods: chocolate, bread, cheese

98. Write yourself motivational sticky notes and post them throughout your home

99. Splurge on a totally offline vacation at your dream destination and leave all the gadgets behind

And finally #100, the most important one of all:

Simply be and savor the rare luxury of doing nothing. Daydream. Sail away. Listen to the breezy beats of "Orinoco Flow" by Enya and she'll serenade you to do the same.

Can you think of ten more offline ideas to enjoy?

AFTERWORD

For the love of trees, join the sharing economy. Loved this book? Give it to your best friend. Hated this book? Give it to someone who gets on your nerves. Thank you. And thank you for contributing to tree planting efforts in the national and state forests of the United States. A portion of the proceeds from each copy sold of *Offline Rebel* will be donated towards nurturing a greener earth.

As this book goes to print, I have lived without that squawking monkey on my back for nearly six months. After improvising for four months without any mobile phone at all, I purchased a $39 vintage feature phone without a data plan. Many people have asked me if my decision is just temporary, a gimmick if you will, to do something groundbreaking and thus be able to write a book about it.

My answer is that I have in fact taken yet another step away from technology since completing this book: I canceled my home Internet service. I still need the Internet to work, but I access it from cafés and libraries rather than my home office which no longer has a landline either since the two technologies were intertwined.

Has the transition been easy? Toronto-based writer Pasquale Casullo also cut the cord on his home Internet and sums it up well:

> Just as dipping into a piping hot bubble bath requires a strong constitution, so does going without home Wi-Fi. But, once in, it is a soothing, relaxing experience.[1]

Indeed, this extra effort to live tech-lite has gifted me with even more time and productivity as I am in the midst of writing my next book. Email me at offlinerebel@outlook.com and I will send you details and updates as they arise!

Now close this book and go live your life, rebel!

ACKNOWLEDGMENTS

This project has been my heartbeat since the day I scribbled my first ideas on a sheet of loose leaf paper. I am immeasurably grateful to all those who supported me in this unconventional endeavor.

Loving thanks to my mother, Joan, for urging me to move forward with *Offline Rebel* during periods of writer's block and for being yourself. You are an inspiration.

Enormous thanks to my best friend who is more family than friend, Maria, for voicing your support of this project from the very beginning. I treasure our sisterhood.

To my Uncle Steve, you have always inspired and supported me. Thank you – and yes, you're still a member of the Nature Club.

My warmest thanks to those who participated in interviews for this book, especially Dr. Bassam Frangieh.

Finally, thank you readers for taking this journey with me. I hope your lives will be richer and bolder as you blaze your own individual paths to peace.

NOTES

Introduction: Birth of a Rebellion

1. Adrian F. Ward, Kristen Duke, Ayelet Gneezy, and Maarten W. Bos, "Brain Drain: The Mere Presence of One's Own Smartphone Reduces Available Cognitive Capacity," *Journal of the Association for Consumer Research*, April 2017.

2. Hilary Andersson, "Social Media Apps Are 'Deliberately' Addictive to Users, *BBC News*, July 4, 2018, bbc.com/news/technology-44640959.

3. Ibid.

4. "Gaming Disorder," World Health Organization, September 2018, who.int/features/qa/gaming-disorder/en/.

PART ONE: RECLAIM THE MAGIC

Chapter 1: What's Your Boldness IQ?

1. Randy Kambic, "Peter Sagal on Running Toward Mindfulness." *Natural Awakenings Sarasota/Manatee Edition* (May 2019): 48.

2. Emily S. Rueb, "W.H.O. Says Limited or No Screen Time

for Children under 5," *The New York Times*, April 24, 2019, nytimes.com/2019/04/24/health/screen-time-kids.html.

3. "Sleep Statistics Reveal the (Shocking) Cost to Health and Society," TheGoodBody.com, December 10, 2018, thegoodbody.com/sleep-statistics/.

4. Neil Postman, *Amusing Ourselves to Death: Public Discourse in the Age of Show Business*, (New York: Penguin Books, Anniversary Edition, 2005), 4.

Chapter 2: Wake the Genius

1. Cal Newport, *Deep Work: Rules for Focused Success in a Distracted World*, (New York: Grand Central Publishing, 2016), 44.

2. Patrick Fissler, Olivia Caroline Küster, Daria Laptinskaya, Laura Sophia Loy, Christine A.F. von Arnim, and Iris-Tatjana Kolassa, "Jigsaw Puzzling Taps Multiple Cognitive Abilities and Is a Potential Protective Factor for Cognitive Aging," *Frontiers in Aging Neuroscience*, 10:299 (2018).

3. "Smartphone Addiction Creates Imbalance in the Brain," Press Release, Radiological Society of North America, November 30, 2017, press.rsna.org/timssnet/media/pressreleases/14_pr_target.cfm?ID=1989.

4. Catherine Price, *How to Break Up with Your Phone: The 30-Day Plan to Take Back Your Life*. (New York: Ten Speed Press, 2018): 7.

5. Ibid, 21.

6. Maureen Callahan, "Our Cell Phones Are Killing Us," *New York Post*, June 18, 2016, nypost.com/2016/06/18/our-cellphones-are-killing-us/.

7. Jenn Sinrich, "30 Amazing Facts About Your Brain That Will Blow Your Mind," *Reader's Digest*, rd.com/health/wellness/brain-facts/. Retrieved August 7, 2019.

8. Deane Alban, "72 Amazing Human Brain Facts (Based on

the Latest Science)," *Be Brain Fit*, April 23, 2019, bebrainfit.com/human-brain-facts/.

Chapter 3: You Have No New Notifications
1. Kurt Schlosser, "Can You Live Without a Smartphone? This Flip Phone Fan Has Done It for 13 Years and Will Teach You How," *GeekWire*, January 16, 2019, geekwire.com/2019/can-live-without-smartphone-flip-phone-fan-done-13-years-will-teach/.
2. Ibid.
3. "How to Survive in Seattle Without a Smartphone," *The Evergrey*, theevergrey.com/newsletter/2019-01-14-how-to-survive-in-seattle-without-a-smartphone/. Retrieved May 30, 2019.
4. Alfred Ng, "Your Smartphones Are Getting More Valuable for Hackers," CNET, March 8, 2018, cnet.com/news/your-smartphones-are-getting-more-valuable-for-hackers/.
5. Geoffrey A. Fowler, "It's the Middle of the Night: Do You Know Who Your iPhone Is Talking to?" *The Washington Post*, May 28, 2019, washingtonpost.com/technolo-gy/2019/05/28/its-middle-night-do-you-know-who-your-iphone-is-talking/?noredirect=on&utm_term=.39399ca85bbe.
6. Geoffrey A. Fowler, "Alexa Has Been Eavesdropping on You This Whole Time," *The Washington Post*, May 6, 2019, washingtonpost.com/technology/2019/05/06/alexa-has-been-eavesdropping-you-this-whole-time/?noredirect=on&utm_term=.7f9189b1d504
7. Alison Grace Johansen, "Is Private Browsing Really Private? Short Answer: No," Norton by Symantec, us.norton.com/in-ternetsecurity-privacy-your-private-browser-is-not-so-private-after-all.html. Retrieved June 22, 2019.
8. Mari Colham, "Why It's Important to Take a Break from Smartphones and Social Media," *Medium*, September 22,

2018, medium.com/datadriveninvestor/why-its-important-to-take-a-break-from-smartphones-and-social-media-b80fbb1f8d2c.

9. Bernard Marr, "How Much Data Do We Create Every Day? The Mind-Blowing Stats Everyone Should Read," *Forbes*, May 21, 2018, forbes.com/sites/bernardmarr/2018/05/21/how-much-data-do-we-create-every-day-the-mind-blowing-stats-everyone-should-read/#4e85c0df60ba.

10. Kelsey Gee, "Sunday Night Is the New Monday Morning and Workers Are Miserable." *Wall Street Journal*, July 7, 2019, wsj.com/articles/sunday-night-is-the-new-monday-morning-and-workers-are-miserable-11562497212.

11. Seth Fiegerman, "Slack Is Ruining My Life and I Love It," CNN Business, June 20, 2019, cnn.com/2019/06/20/tech/slack-confessions/index.html.

12. Sissi Cao, "Nokia Reissues Iconic 'Banana Phone' Held by Keanu Reeves in 'The Matrix'," *Observer*, February 26, 2018, observer.com/2018/02/nokia-reissues-banana-phone-keanu-reeves-matrix/.

13. Ingrid Lunden, "Nokia 8110's Slider 'Matrix' Feature Phone Returns with 4G and a €79 Price Tag," TechCrunch, February 25, 2018, techcrunch.com/2018/02/25/nokia-8110s-slider-matrix-feature-phone-returns-with-4g-and-a-e79-price-tag/?ncid=mobilenavtrend.

Chapter 4: Books & Blurbs

1. Naomi Baron, "Why Digital Reading Is No Substitute for Print," *New Republic*, July 20, 2016, newrepublic.com/article/135326/digital-reading-no-substitute-print.

2. "Computer Vision Syndrome," American Optometric Association, aoa.org/patients-and-public/caring-for-your-vision/protecting-your-vision/computer-vision-syndrome. Retrieved June 3, 2019.

3. Naomi Baron, "Why Digital Reading Is No Substitute for

Print," *New Republic*, July 20, 2016, newrepublic.com/article/135326/digital-reading-no-substitute-print.

4. Markham Heed, "You Asked: Is It Bad for You to Read the News Constantly?" *Time*, January 31, 2018, time.com/5125894/is-reading-news-bad-for-you/.

5. Ibid.

Chapter 5: Connect the Dots

1. Connie Guglielmo, "10 Years Ago Today: Remembering Steve Jobs Make iPhone History," CNET, January 9, 2017, cnet.com/news/iphone-at-10-apple-steve-jobs-make-iphone-history-remembering/.

2. Mireille Guiliano, *French Women for All Seasons*. (New York: Alfred A. Knopf, 2006): 109.

3. Stephanie Mlot, "Study: College Students Choose Smartphones over Food," Geek.com, December 3, 2018, geek.com/tech/study-college-students-choose-smartphones-over-food-1763856/.

4. Eric Pickersgill, "Removed: Project Statement," ericpickersgill.com/removed. Retrieved May 21, 2019.

5. Ibid.

6. Jane Ridley, "One in Ten People Checks Their Phone during Sex: Survey)," *New York Post*, June 7, 2018, nypost.com/2018/06/07/one-in-10-people-checks-their-phone-during-sex-survey/.

7. Susan Biali Haas, M.D., "6 Ways that Night-time Phone Use Destroys Your Sleep," *Psychology Today*, April 17, 2018, psychologytoday.com/us/blog/prescriptions-life/201804/6-ways-night-time-phone-use-destroys-your-sleep.

8. Tony Reinke, *12 Ways Your Phone Is Changing You* (Wheaton, IL: Crossway, 2017), 198.

Chapter 6: Rearview Mirror

1. Maureen Callahan, "Our Cell Phones Are Killing Us," *New*

York Post, June 18, 2016, nypost.com/2016/06/18/our-cellphones-are-killing-us/.

2. Nancy Colier, *The Power of Off: The Mindful Way to Stay Sane in a Virtual World*, (Boulder, CO: Sounds True, 2016), 113.

3. "'Selfie' Named by Oxford Dictionaries as Word of 2013," *BBC News*, November 19, 2013, bbc.com/news/uk-24992393.

4. Mike Wendling, "Does This 90-year Old Photo Show the World's First Selfie Stick?" *BBC Trending*, December 19, 2014, bbc.com/news/blogs-trending-30550998.

5. Sasha Lekach and Suzanne Ciechalski, "Don't Even Think About Bringing Your Selfie Stick to These Tourist Destinations," mashable.com, July 29, 2017, mashable.com/2017/07/29/selfie-sticks-banned-travel-tourist-destinations/.

6. Eric Dodds, "Selfie Stick to Be Banned from Disney World Theme Parks," *Time*, June 26, 2015, time.com/3938078/disney-world-selfie-stick-ban/

7. Mandi Woodruff, "Why This Controversial German Woman Turned Her Back on Money for 16 Years," *Business Insider*, June 18, 2012, businessinsider.com/how-heidemarie-schwermer-has-lived-without-money-for-16-years-2012-6.

8. Ibid.

9. AFP, "Indy/Life," *The Independent*, August 20, 2011, independent.co.uk/life-style/happiness-is-a-life-without-money-in-rich-germany-2341025.html.

10. Age of Happiness, "Heidemarie Schwermer, Who Doesn't Need Money," Medium.com, May 3, 2016, medium.com/@ageofhappiness/heidemarie-schwermer-who-doesnt-need-money-f701e2879945.

PART TWO: CREATE NEW MAGIC

Chapter 7: Screen-Free Living Spree

1. Uptin Saiidi, "Silent Retreat: What a 3-Day Digital Detox Did for Me," CNBC, May 23, 2019, cnbc.com/2019/05/23/silent-retreat-what-a-3-day-digital-detox-did-for-me.html.
2. Nicholas Carr, *The Shallows: What the Internet Is Doing to Our Brains*. (New York: W.W. Norton & Company, 2011), 3.
3. Adrienne LaFrance, "A Search for the Zombie Websites of 1995," *The Atlantic*, April 21, 2017, theatlantic.com/technology/archive/2017/04/a-search-for-the-zombie-websites-of-1995/523848/.

Chapter 8: Velvet Joy

1. Susan Casey, *Voices in the Ocean: A Journey into the Wild and Haunting World of Dolphins*. (New York: Doubleday, 2015), 19.
2. Stephanie Marohn, *What the Animals Taught Me*. (Charlottesville, VA: Hampton Roads Publishing Company, Inc., 2012), 89-90.

Chapter 9: Emerald Green

1. Rhett Palmer, "Digital Cocaine: A Journey Toward iBalance, Interview of Author Brad Huddleston," *Vero's Voice* (June 2019) Issue 101: 6.
2. "Children in Nature," National Recreation and Park Association, nrpa.org/uploadedFiles/nrpa.org/Advocacy/Children-in-Nature.pdf. Retrieved June 17, 2019.
3. Harriet Sherwood, "Getting Back to Nature: How Forest Bathing Can Make Us Feel Better," *The Guardian*, June 8, 2019, theguardian.com/environment/2019/jun/08/forest-bathing-japanese-practice-in-west-wellbeing.
4. Hannah Jane Parkinson, "Kate's Forest Bathing, Harry's Meditating: Wellness Is a Right Royal Fad," *The Guardian*, January 16, 2019, theguardian.com/uk-news/shortcuts/2019/jan/16/wellness-now-right-royal-fad.

5. Dr. Qing Li, *Forest Bathing: How Trees Can Help You Find Health and Happiness.* (New York: Viking, 2018), 15.

6. Ibid, 112.

7. Ibid, 164.

8. "How to Recycle Old Electronics," *Consumer Reports*, April 22, 2018, consumerreports.org/recycling/how-to-recycle-electronics/.

9. Kay Vandette, "Smartphone Manufacturing Is Brutal on the Environment," Earth.com, August 30, 2018, earth.com/news/smartphone-manufacturing-brutal-environment/.

10. "Cell Phone Toxins and the Harmful Effects on the Human Body When Recycled Improperly," e-Cycle, October 15, 2013, e-cycle.com/cell-phone-toxins-and-the-harmful-effects-on-the-human-body-when-recycled-improperly/.

11. Mark Wilson, "Smartphones Are Killing the Planet Faster Than Anyone Expected," *Fast Company*, March 27, 2018, fastcompany.com/90165365/smartphones-are-wrecking-the-planet-faster-than-anyone-expected.

12. Ibid.

Chapter 10: Artist's Cobblestone Path

1. Anne Morrow Lindbergh, *Gift from the Sea: 50th Anniversary Edition*, (New York: Pantheon Books, 2005), 36.

2. Reeve Lindbergh, *Introduction to the 50th Anniversary Edition of Gift from the Sea*, (New York: Pantheon Books, 2005), ix.

3. Anne LaBastille, *Woodswoman: Living Alone in the Adirondack Wilderness*, (New York: Penguin Books, 1976), 22-23.

4. Justin Housman, "Anne LaBastille May Have Out-Thoreau'd Thoreau," *Adventure Journal*, October 11, 2018, adventure-journal.com/2018/10/anne-labastille-may-have-out-thoreaud-thoreau/.

5. Tim Palmer, "Personal Statement," timpalmer.org/personal_statement. Retrieved July 29, 2019.

6. Megan Leonhardt, "This Millennial Will Give Up a Smartphone for a Year to Win $100,000 in the Vitaminwater Challenge," CNBC, February 15, 2019, cnbc.com/2019/02/14/millennial-gives-up-smartphone-to-win-100000-dollars-in-vitaminwater-challenge.html.

7. Elana A. Mugdan @officialdragonspeaker, Instagram, "If Your Heart Is Broken, This Book Is for You," July 17 2019, instagram.com/p/B0B7-0tJAE0/?utm_source=ig_web_copy_link. Retrieved July 18, 2019.

8. Ibid.

Chapter 11: Mind & Body in Synch

1. Paige Leskin, "American Kids Want to Be Famous on YouTube and Kids in China Want to Go to Space: Survey," *Business Insider*, July 19, 2019, businessinsider.com/american-kids-youtube-star-astronauts-survey-2019-7.

2. Dr. Patrizia Collard, *Journey into Mindfulness: Gentle Ways to Let Go of Stress and Live in the Moment*, (London, UK: Bounty Books, 2015), 59.

3. Marianne Williamson, *A Return to Love: Reflections on the Principles of "A Course in Miracles,"* (New York: HarperCollins, 1992).

4. Jennie Cohen, "7 Things You May Not Know About the Sistine Chapel," History.com, November 1, 2012, history.com/news/7-things-you-may-not-know-about-the-sistine-chapel.

5. Serina Sandhu, "Denmark Ranked Happiest Country in the World for the Third Time – How Did Your Country Do?" *The Independent*, March 16, 2016, independent.co.uk/news/world/europe/denmark-happiest-country-for-third-time-united-nations-report-a6934196.html.

6. Kelsey Glennon, "How to Create a Hygge Campsite," *Outdoorsy Never Idle Journal*, July 27, 2018, outdoorsy.com/blog/how-to-create-a-hygge-campsite.

7. Isaac Stanley-Becker, "'Horns Are Growing on Young People's Skulls: Phone Use Is to Blame, Research Suggests," *Washington Post*, June 25, 2019, washingtonpost.com/nation/2019/06/20/horns-are-growing-young-peoples-skulls-phone-use-is-blame-research-suggests/?noredirect=on&utm_term=.b1b65a16c332.

8. Joanne Cavanaugh Simpson, "Digital Disabilities – Text Neck, Cellphone Elbow – Are Painful and Growing," *Washington Post*, June 13, 2016, washingtonpost.com/national/health-science/digital-disabilities--text-neck-cellphone-elbow--are-painful-and-growing/2016/06/13/df070c7c-0afd-11e6-a6b6-2e6de3695b0e_story.html?noredirect=on&utm_term=.7dcdb17117b3.

Chapter 12: The Golden Egg

1. Laure Dugas, *Champagne Baby: How One Parisian Learned to Love Wine – and Life – the American Way*, (New York: Ballantine Books, 2016), 308.

PART THREE: LIVE YOUR MAGIC

The Ultimate Challenge

1. Kif Leswing, "Billionaire Warren Buffett, a Major Apple Investor, Uses a $20 Flip Phone," CNBC, March 28, 2019, cnbc.com/2019/03/28/billionaire-warren-buffett-a-major-apple-investor-uses-a-20-flip-phone.html.

Afterword

1. Pasquale Casullo, "Why I Refuse to Have the Internet in My Home," *The Globe and Mail*, November 14, 2018, theglobeandmail.com/life/first-person/article-why-i-refuse-to-have-the-internet-in-my-home/.

Printed in Poland
by Amazon Fulfillment
Poland Sp. z o.o., Wrocław

31878962R00115